How to Beat

Fears and Phobias

One Step at a Time

How to Beat

Fears and Phobias

One Step at a Time

Mark Papworth

ROBINSON

ROBINSON

First published in Great Britain in 2020 by Robinson

1 3 5 7 9 10 8 6 4 2

A CIP catalogue record for this book
is available from the British Library.

ISBN: 978-1-47214-399-0

Typeset in Minion by Initial Typesetting Services, Edinburgh
Printed and bound in Great Britain by Clays Ltd, Elcograf S.p.A.

Papers used by Robinson are from well-managed forests
and other responsible sources.

Robinson
An imprint of
Little, Brown Book Group
Carmelite House
50 Victoria Embankment
London EC4Y 0DZ

An Hachette UK Company
www.hachette.co.uk

www.littlebrown.co.uk

CONTENTS

GETTING GOING

Well done for making the first step!

I am really glad that you have reached out and started reading this book! In doing so, you have taken the first and one of the most important steps on your journey to recovery. Often, in order to get better, we first have to reach a point where we are willing to invest quite a bit of time and energy into this task. This is because psychological treatments usually involve a great deal of personal effort. This is needed to reap the full benefit of what they have to offer. So, just before we start, can I check that you have this time and effort available? I'll talk more about this later in this chapter.

Let's start by thinking about some of the terms that I will use in this book and the experience of phobias. A 'fear' is an unpleasant emotion that we all experience when we believe that we are threatened in some way. 'Anxiety' tends to be associated with a vaguer or more diffuse sense of threat, perhaps something that might happen in the future. On the other hand, fear is usually associated with a clear and obvious threat, for example a person with a big knife coming towards us in a dark alley. A 'phobia' is a psychological disorder that consists of marked and persistent fear which significantly impacts upon lifestyle or results in significant distress. You can see that these concepts overlap quite a bit so I will tend to use 'anxiety', 'fear' and 'phobia' interchangeably within the book.

Experiencing a phobia means that at times you can experience overwhelming fear. Alternatively, you may be avoiding situations that might trigger fear because you worry that you will not be able to cope with them. In this way, fear can act as a kind of mental prison that limits your life. It may have a number of consequences on your daily routines. You may have tried to overcome your fear before and have not succeeded. It may be that others who care about you have offered you well-meaning advice that has not allowed you to make any progress, despite you doing your very best to follow it. At this point, you may feel hopeless about your situation. Because of this, I have written the book in several short sections that will allow you to address your phobia, one step at a time and at a pace that is manageable for you, and in a way that should allow you to get control and hope back in your life.

This book is designed to help people who experience most kinds of phobias. However, there are a few exceptions that usually require a different or an extra form of treatment. The first of these is a phobia that revolves around the sight of blood and having injections. This provokes a very different response to the 'fight or flight' response described in Section 2 of this book and so needs a different form of treatment. The second is a phobia of social situations where the person is worried about others' perceptions of them. They worry that they will be embarrassed or humiliated. This is a more complex form of phobia. Another more complex form of phobia is 'agoraphobia'. Here the focus of the fear is a need to escape, usually in case the person experiences severe panic symptoms but also because of other worrying consequences as well. It can cause the individual to avoid situations such as crowded or enclosed spaces, as well as public transport. Whilst the 'graded exposure' technique described in this book may be of some help for these 'complex phobias', often some other strategies or additional supports are needed for the person to make a full recovery. For instance, there is another book in this series that teaches individuals how to cope with panic disorder (*How to Beat Panic Disorder One Step at a Time*).

This book includes two case examples of people who

have used the techniques described here to understand the nature of their fear and get back control
of their lives. These are fictitious characters but are
based on the stories of real patients. These examples
illustrate how people have used the techniques within their daily lives to help them to overcome their
fear. The techniques I will teach you have been used
by health professionals to help people to overcome
their fears for over half a century. This means that
they have been tried, tested, refined and tested over
and over again. In fact, researchers have concluded
that the use of these techniques for tackling phobias
produces better results than other psychological
treatments for this particular problem.

About myself

First of all, I would like to introduce myself. We are
going to work together for a few weeks so it might
be helpful if you know a little about me. Hopefully
this will help you to build a picture of me in your
'mind's eye'. I am a consultant clinical psychologist
who has, for over thirty years, been helping people
with very similar issues to you. For the most part,
I have provided psychological therapy to people in
community health centres and doctors' surgeries
(called 'GP Practices' in the UK). Whilst doing
this, I have also worked for over twenty years at

Newcastle University which is one of the most re-
spected universities in the UK. Here I was involved
in the training of clinical psychologists before
dedicating my time to developing a training in a
new 'low intensity' form of Cognitive Behavioural
Therapy (see more on this below). I also do research
into how best to help individuals through the use
of self-help materials and into what people require
from psychological services. Outside of work, I enjoy spending time with my partner Danna. We love
eating out (my biggest indulgence is food), going
to the cinema and seeing shows. At the weekends
we enjoy cycling in the local countryside, usually
nearby in Northumberland, County Durham or the
Lake District.

What is Cognitive Behavioural Therapy?

This book is based on an evidence-based psychological therapy called Cognitive Behavioural Therapy
(or 'CBT' for short). The evidence supporting this
approach comes from many research trials which
are summarised into important scientific reviews.
These reviews say that CBT is effective for lots of
people who experience anxiety difficulties (including phobias) and also depression. Of course,
sometimes people with an anxiety disorder will

become depressed as well, due to the consequences of experiencing anxiety.

CBT can be provided in a face-to-face format (with a therapist in a clinic room) and also in a self-help format such as provided by this book. Sometimes you can also get support whilst using self-help from your doctor or another healthcare professional. The use of CBT self-help books as part of treatment is referred to as 'low intensity CBT'. It is called low intensity because, through this method, people generally require shorter and fewer sessions in their treatment than otherwise with the usual (or 'high intensity') form of CBT. Self-help is recommended for individuals with milder disorders. Everyone with a psychological disorder tends to feel that it affects a huge part of who they are. However, relatively speaking, a milder problem will have less impact on a person's life. If you have a milder phobia, you are more likely to get the maximum benefit from the treatment approach described in this book. I will explain more about this approach in Sections 2 and 3.

Using self-help

One of the advantages of self-help is that you can use the tools described within the book at a pace that best suits you. Saying that, similarly to taking a course of medicine, the approach works best if you keep going with it consistently rather than try it for a bit, have a rest for a month and then pick it up again. Self-help is also an empowering approach in that you will know that the benefit that you have gained has been through *your* own strength and efforts alone.

CBT is mentioned quite often in the popular media such as in magazines or newspapers, and so you may already be familiar with some of its principles. However, if this is your first experience of CBT self-help, flicking through this book may seem a bit daunting. This is understandable. You may worry about what lies ahead. Try not to. I have done my best to make this book as easy as possible to read and use, and have followed what I know to be best practice in writing self-help books.

How to use this book

I have just mentioned that the approach works best if you apply this treatment consistently. However, this doesn't mean that you have to read the whole book in one go! Rather, quite the opposite. The treatment is best done in stages and, for each individual, these stages may take a different length of time.

However, a ball park figure for the whole treatment, depending on how severe your phobia is, will need you to be able to invest around one hour to ninety minutes, at least three times a week for around six to twelve weeks. The sections should allow you to pace yourself, like a mountain climber may break down a climb into several sections, to make it more manageable.

It may be that a healthcare professional has recommended this self-help book to you and you are working through it together. If this is the case, they will be able to answer any questions that you might have, offer you additional advice and may even be able to coach you in completing the exercises. If you are embarking on this treatment on your own, you may wish to highlight helpful sections of text with a marker or make notes in the margin as you go along. Some people find this really helpful. If you are not sure about something, remember that another advantage of using a self-help book is that you can simply go back and read that section again. If you need to do this, please don't become frustrated or self-critical. The most important thing, from my perspective, is that you understand the techniques that are described within the book.

Overview of the book

Some people like to read through the whole book first and then go back and start using the techniques. Others prefer to use the techniques straight away after reading a section. Whatever you find to be the most helpful is fine. However, the key thing is that when you are ready, you put the techniques into practice in your daily life. You may need to reorder your schedule for a few weeks to allow this to happen. Within the book, there are activities that prepare you for this. Complete the activities as you work through it. I have broken down the book into five sections and you can move through the book in a way that you feel will be the most helpful for you.

You may wish to start your treatment by hearing about how other people have used the approach to help them to overcome their phobias. This can provide a brief overview of the treatment and may boost your confidence before committing to changes yourself. If so, turn to the two recovery stories in Section 5. Here, Sarah and Azid share what they did to beat their phobias. When you have finished Section 5 you can turn back and work through the rest of the book. Alternatively, you may be more inclined to start by learning more about the techniques involved in the treatment. If so, then I would suggest that you work through the book in order from start to finish.

Sections of the book

Section 1: Getting going (page 1)

In this section, I will help you to understand what fear, anxiety and phobias are. There are stories and tips from other people who have used this approach, to help you to get started and to keep you going. You will also get a chance to set some personal goals, which will help you to track your progress.

Section 2: Understanding fears and phobias (page 33)

Here you will learn all about fear; how it is the body's way of protecting you, and how to overcome it naturally. You will learn how fears are maintained and how to break the vicious cycles that can be created when fear takes over.

Section 3: Graded exposure treatment (page 61)

Using the tools within this section, you will learn how to plan a treatment programme to help you to get on top of your fear. You will be guided in carrying out your plan and be able to review the results and any progress made. I will also help you to troubleshoot any hiccups that you may encounter along the way.

Section 4: The relapse prevention toolkit (page 97)

Once you are feeling better, we will look at ways to ensure that you maintain the progress that you have made. This will involve reviewing what you have learnt and making a plan for the future.

Section 5: Recovery stories (page 129)

Finally, you can catch up with the people that you first met in Section 1. Here, they share their stories of having a phobia and describe what they did in order to help themselves. You can see how they put their plans into action and continued to stay on top of their fear.

Top tips before you get going

Before beginning to understand fears and phobias and how these affect you, I would like to share with you some top tips about the use of self-help books. These come from both people who have benefited from CBT self-help to overcome their difficulties and from health professionals who support people in using CBT self-help.

Top tip 1: Give it your best shot

'I had tried to face my fear before but, as the book gave me a clear path forward, I was really able to push myself harder this time and commit to the treatment.'

It is unlikely that this treatment will be completely plain sailing. There may be some challenges for you. The treatment requires that you confront some situations in a controlled and paced manner. It is important that you give the treatment your best shot and work through these. Think of this as a bit like going to the dentist. No one enjoys this experience, but most people regularly endure it because they understand that, despite the discomfort, it is helpful in the long run. If things seem too much, turn to the troubleshooting guide in Section 3 or read the case examples in Section 5. Revisiting these case examples can be helpful in motivating you. If a healthcare professional is supporting you, they can help in troubleshooting. They may be able to check that you are using the techniques correctly and also offer encouragement.

Top tip 2: Put what you have learned into action

> 'Once I understood the treatment, for a few weeks, rather than go to the gym every evening, I alternated trips to the gym with doing the exercises in the book. One day I did one, the next day I did the other.'

Individuals only gain benefit from therapy if it results in change in their life. A therapist or self-help materials can only offer the guidance and tools needed for this: it is up to you to put them into action. Generally speaking, with therapies such as CBT, the more effort people put into the therapy, the greater they benefit. In this way, after doing some reading, putting these tools and techniques into action is the key to feeling better. Think of it as being a bit like learning to play the piano. The teacher offers the instruction, but it is up to the pupil to put in the practice. Without investing time into this, the pupil is unlikely to progress very much in between the lessons. The lessons alone don't make someone proficient.

Top tip 3: Writing in the book is allowed – in fact it is encouraged!

> 'As I improved, I looked back on my records and I could really see how much I had progressed.'

As part of this treatment it is really important that you remember the tools and techniques that are described in this book. Also, I will help you to make some plans for your treatment which you will need to remember as well. To help with this, I would like to wholeheartedly invite you to write in this book. To make this easier for you, each time that you are invited to do some writing, I have included this image. When you see it, it is a reminder to put pen to paper. As well as helping you in your treatment, writing things down can really boost confidence by allowing you to look back later and see the progress that you have made. If you prefer to use a pad, journal or smartphone, that is, of course, also fine.

Top tip 4: Like everyone, expect to have both good and bad days

'I learned that as I am in charge of my own treatment, I could always "dial" things back a little if a step seemed too difficult for me.'

Within your treatment, I hope that everything will go smoothly for you. For many
people this is generally the case. However, it
is not uncommon to have the odd setback.
Within this book, I will encourage you to
think about these in terms of opportunities
for problem solving rather than experiences
of failure. As you understand how you react
in different situations, you will be able to
fine-tune the treatment to allow you to continue to make progress. I will help you to do
this in the troubleshooting section within
Section 3.

Top tip 5: Act according to your goals rather because of how you feel

'It felt really difficult, not letting my fear
drive how I acted. However, when I resisted
this, I saw that my confidence increased,
and it was easier to do it again.'

A main focus for the book is to act according
to your goals and targets, not how you think
or feel. In fact, this book will ask you, in a
graded and controlled fashion, to react in
the opposite way to old patterns which have
been established because of your feelings. I
will, therefore, ask you to set some goals a
bit later in this section. You will read more
about the patterns that maintain phobias and

how to break these in Sections 2 and 3. These insights are a key to starting to get on top of your fear. So, try not to listen to your body when you become fearful. Try not to let manageable levels of fear stop you from either completing this treatment or doing other things that you need or want to do. For example, we have all experienced some anxiety or fear going to the doctor or attending an interview. It would be very limiting if we always avoided these kinds of situations. In Section 3, I will show you how to overcome your fear in a manageable fashion.

Top tip 6: Let your doctor know that you are going to use this book

'I went to see Dr Chen. I told her about my plans and showed her the book. She said that as I was undergoing treatment, she would reduce the dose of my medication. She said that she wanted to see me for more regular appointments to check on how I am doing.'

There should be no medical reason to stop you from using the techniques in this book. However, the exercises will ask you to do things that will stimulate a level of controlled discomfort. Also, medications that are prescribed for psychological problems (as well as other substances such as alcohol) can interfere with the treatment. For these reasons, I recommend that you make your doctor (or other healthcare provider) aware before engaging with the exposure activities that are described in Section 3, to talk through how this might be best managed. I talk more about this issue on page 69.

Top tip 7: Involve family and friends if you can

'I told Jenny about my fear of dogs and that I was getting help for it. She offered to come over with a friend's dog if it would be helpful for the treatment.'

There are many ways that involving others in your treatment can be useful, providing of course that they are supportive in nature rather than impatient or critical. For example, just the process of letting others know that you have committed to undertake the treatment can make you more likely to carry it through. In telling others, you have made yourself more publicly accountable for your actions. On another level, involving others can mean that they can support you through their encouragement. Allowing others to read through this book with you may facilitate this. If they share with you knowledge of the treatment, they may be able to help you with any troubleshooting that might be required. Most importantly, sometimes others' input may be essential for you to be able to carry out some of the tasks that will be involved in your treatment (you will see others' involvement in some tasks within Sarah and Azid's 'ladders' described in Section 3).

Top tip 8: Set time aside to use the book and use reminders

'I set a phone alert to remind me to put the book in my bag and take it with me on my journey to work. I can then read it on the bus.'

Many people report struggling or forgetting to carry out their treatment because of their busy lives. People also put off the tasks involved in treatment because they feel that they are a little difficult. This is a natural tendency that is termed 'procrastination'. With this in mind, I strongly advise you to set cues or reminders to help you to follow through with the treatment tasks. This may involve some planning and moving things around in your day, just for the few weeks over which the treatment will take place. This is another reason to involve others (Top tip 7). Sometimes they can help to take over a commitment temporarily to allow you to have some additional time to enable you to focus on your treatment. Think about how you organise your life at the moment. Perhaps you use a calendar on the kitchen wall, a paper diary or an electronic diary on your smartphone. Incorporate the tasks that are involved in your treatment into this system. Start the habit now by scheduling some time into your diary over the next few days to allow you to continue to read this book.

Getting and using support

At times, you may feel like giving up the treatment. This is perfectly normal and to be expected. It is part of the pattern that is likely to be fuelling your fear. In the next section, I will explain how avoidance is the main way that phobias are maintained. In this way, it is perfectly understandable that you may be tempted to fall back on this approach. However, these feelings will pass. Think about what you have lost because of your phobia and what you will reclaim if you are able to overcome it. If you get stuck, you can 'regroup' by looking at the troubleshooting guide in Section 3 of this book. Beware of trying to achieve too much too quickly – remember the story of the tortoise and the hare! If you keep moving step by step, eventually you should reach your destination. A journey of several miles starts with those first steps. If you keep stepping, you should get there in the end.

It may be that you are already receiving support from your doctor or another healthcare professional. In several countries, it is now possible to receive support from a healthcare professional who is specially trained in motivating and supporting people in working through CBT self-help. These people are often called psychological wellbeing practitioners (or 'PWPs' for short) or low intensity workers/ coaches. England has an Improving Access to Psychological Therapies (IAPT) programme. This allows people who are suitable for CBT self-help and who are struggling with anxiety or low mood to be supported in the National Health Service (NHS). They can either see a PWP in a therapy setting or speak to them over the telephone. If you are receiving support from a PWP, it is likely that you will be speaking to them regularly to:

- Guide you in completing the tasks in this book.

- Help you to identify and solve any problems that you might encounter along the way.

- Answer any questions that you may have.

They will also be able to guide you in how to get help if you have one of the phobias I mentioned earlier which needs a different form of treatment. In England, to find out more about your local IAPT/ NHS service, use this phrase in a search engine: 'find psychological therapies (IAPT) services'. Alternatively, this link works at the time I am writing this book:

https://www.nhs.uk/service-search/find-a-psycho logical-therapies-service

You may not be receiving support to use this book, or you may live in an area where this kind of support is not available. If you feel that you need support, talk to your doctor who may have access to other services that can offer you a similar form of help. You can also find an accredited local CBT therapist who works in the UK through this page:

https://www.babcp.com/Public/Accessing-CBT. aspx

Of course, you may wish to work through this book on your own, or with the support of a friend or family member. That is also fine. Please just keep in mind that professional support should be available to you if you need it and that having someone to support you can, for some people, mean that they are more likely to complete the treatment.

There are no rules about how quickly you should move through the book. Indeed, it is better to take things steadily and have repeated experiences of success, rather than attempt to move on too quickly and risk having setbacks. There are no definite expectations around the amount of time it will take for you to complete the treatment. This will depend on factors such as the time that you are able to invest in the treatment and the nature of your phobia. However, for the book to be successful, I would ask you to commit to two things:

1. Give it a go: Read it and do it!

Give the activities a go and see what works for you. The more that you can put things into practice, the more likely it is that you will benefit from the treatment. Remember that we all have days when we feel like giving up. Make a commitment to use the book and put things into practice, even if you are uncertain that it will work for you before your attempt. Make a deal with yourself to give the treatment your best shot for six weeks and see how you feel after this point.

2. If things get really bad and you think about ending your life, speak to someone straight away

For a few people, when they are experiencing emotional difficulties and things begin to get on top of them, they can feel so bad that they think about ending their life. They sometimes start to make plans to carry this out. If things get so bad that you are having these thoughts frequently or plan to harm yourself in any way, get help now! There are details of support agencies listed in the back of this book (pages 186–8), some of which you can contact twenty-four hours a day. Let your doctor or other healthcare professional know how you feel. They can help. Tell someone else, such as a trusted friend or family member. They may be able to support you in getting help. Remember that you won't always feel this way and that there are things that you can do to feel better.

Feeling suicidal, at times, is commonly part of the experience of hopelessness or depression. These can be treated directly or can lift as improvements start to occur as a consequence of your phobia treatment. When individuals recover in this way, they no longer feel like ending their life. If you frequently feel depressed, it may be helpful to seek treatment for your depression first and then, when you are feeling better in your mood, you will be better placed to start the treatment described in this book. If this reflects how you are feeling, it is really important to discuss this with your doctor.

Making change happen

Many people, who would otherwise struggle to get going with their treatment, have found the following activity to be helpful as it focuses their mind. Complete the questions in the box below to focus your attention on change. You can write as much or as little as you like. Then I will help you to set the goals that you want to work on.

How important is it for me to change? Write down all of the ways that your problem has limited your life to date. Additionally, write how your problem might impact upon your life in the future if it remains unchecked or even worsens. How will it interfere with you achieving your goals? What have you had to sacrifice for this problem? Imagine that you go to sleep tonight, and you wake up tomorrow and everything in your life was how you wanted it to be, with fear no longer being a problem for you. Write down below what your life would look like if this happened.

....

....

....

....

....

Do I have the opportunity to change? I want you to imagine that this treatment may take, for the sake of argument, around ninety minutes a day, for three days a week, for eight weeks. To be able to prioritise your treatment for these two months, what needs to change in your life? Are there some commitments that you can do less often? Is there some extra support that you can enlist temporarily? Remember also that we spoke earlier about the use of calendar reminders? Write down what you can put into place to allow you to give yourself the best chance of completing the treatment.

....

....

....

....

....

Thinking ahead

In the last exercise I asked you to consider what your life would look like if it was no longer affected by a phobia. Now I would like you to think a little about the process of achieving this and getting the life you want. The way to do this is to break things down into more manageable and focused goals that you would like to achieve over the next few months. These may be associated with the things that you used to do but have had to stop doing, or new things that you would like to do in the future that are currently not possible. Try to make these goals:

1. **Specific.** For example, rather than setting a goal 'to be happy', think about what in particular is missing from your life that means that you are not happy and that you might want to reintroduce in the future. One instance of this might be, for instance, someone with a dog phobia being able to walk in the park or the countryside without being fearful of dogs.

2. **Capable of being measured so that you can record your progress.** Being happy is quite difficult to measure, but you can easily determine whether or not you are walking in the countryside again.

3. **Realistic for you to achieve.** Someone who is afraid of heights may set a goal of going up the New York Empire State Building without experiencing any fear. Realistically, most people will experience a 'healthy' level of fear whilst being at such a height! Also, it is really difficult to get to New York unless you live in the northeastern states of the USA. A more realistic goal might involve a local target that is currently limiting your lifestyle in some meaningful way, such as being able to park your car on any level that you want in a multi-storey car park or walk over high bridges.

When you have decided on the goals that are involved in you feeling better, rate each one regarding how far you can achieve the goal now, then you can come back and rerate them in one, two and three months' time to measure your progress.

My goals for feeling better

Goal 1: ....

....

....

I can do this now   (Today's date___/___/___)
(circle a number):

   0   1   2   3   4   5   6

Not at all   Occasionally   Often   Any time

One-month rerating   (date___/___/___)
(circle a number):

   0   1   2   3   4   5   6

Not at all   Occasionally   Often   Any time

Two-month rerating   (date___/___/___)
(circle a number):

   0   1   2   3   4   5   6

Not at all   Occasionally   Often   Any time

Three-month rerating   (date___/___/___)
(circle a number):

0	1	2	3	4	5	6
Not at all		Occasionally		Often		Any time

Goal 2: ....

....

....

I can do this now   (Today's date___/___/___)
(circle a number):

0	1	2	3	4	5	6
Not at all		Occasionally		Often		Any time

One-month rerating   (date___/___/___)
(circle a number):

0	1	2	3	4	5	6
Not at all		Occasionally		Often		Any time

Two-month rerating   (date___/___/___)
(circle a number):

0	1	2	3	4	5	6
Not at all		Occasionally		Often		Any time

Three-month rerating   (date___/___/___)
(circle a number):

0	1	2	3	4	5	6
Not at all		Occasionally		Often		Any time

Goal 3: ....

....

....

I can do this now   (Today's date___/___/___)
(circle a number):

0	1	2	3	4	5	6
Not at all		Occasionally		Often		Any time

One-month rerating   (date___/___/___)
(circle a number):

0	1	2	3	4	5	6
Not at all		Occasionally		Often		Any time

Two-month rerating   (date___/___/___)
(circle a number):

0	1	2	3	4	5	6
Not at all		Occasionally		Often		Any time

Three-month rerating   (date___/___/___)
(circle a number):

0   1   2   3   4   5   6
Not at all   Occasionally   Often   Any time

You have now considered what your life would be like if you can make changes, and you have set some relevant goals for therapy. Earlier, you began to make some plans regarding how you are going to schedule in the time to begin your treatment. I hope that you now feel really motivated and ready to start. In Section 2, I am going to help you to understand the nature of fear and phobias. This will then lead us into talking about how to overcome them in Section 3.

UNDERSTANDING FEARS AND PHOBIAS

People with phobias often ask themselves questions like:

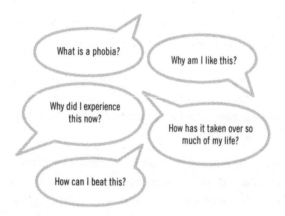

What is a phobia?

Why am I like this?

Why did I experience this now?

How has it taken over so much of my life?

How can I beat this?

In this section, I will look at key information about fears and phobias and answer all of these questions. I will then look at the ways in which a fear or phobia is affecting your life.

Often people request help for a psychological problem because of:

- How they feel ('I feel frightened'). Feelings are usually described in one word (for example, terrified, depressed, anxious or angry).

- Changes in their lifestyle or behaviour – what extra that they have had to do to cope ('I am drinking more alcohol') or what they cannot do anymore ('I can't manage to go to work').

- Physical symptoms occurring in their body ('my heart is racing' or 'my palms are clammy').

- Patterns in their thinking ('sometimes I think that I cannot go on coping like this').

CBT assumes that all of these areas are connected and affect each other. Our understanding of fears and phobias is helped by understanding how these connections work.

Whilst the impact of phobias will affect each of these areas in a similar way, everyone's symptoms will be different and unique. It is quite normal for everyone to feel fear at certain points, for instance just before a job interview or whilst looking over the edge of a high balcony. A full phobia will only develop in a smaller number of people. Whilst your story will be unique to you, in this section I will next introduce

you to Sarah and Azid. They will tell you more of their stories later in this section and also in Section 5. Hopefully, over the course of the book, they will give you some insight into:

- The connections between these symptom areas.

- The challenges faced by some people who experience a phobia.

- What they did to overcome them.

The function of fear

Stories of people with a phobia

I would like to introduce you to two people who have shared their experience of both having a phobia and their use of CBT self-help. The techniques covered in this book really helped them to feel better. Many people have found that reading the stories of others who have both experienced and recovered from a phobia is useful and encouraging.

Sarah is a twenty-three-year-old single mother with a phobia of spiders. When she became a mother, this phobia interfered with her ability to look after her toddler fully. She sought help after she was unable to go near the cot to comfort her crying son when she saw that a spider was on it.

Azid is a forty-two-year-old travelling salesman. He has a phobia of driving over bridges which is interfering with his ability to work. He plans all of his journeys ahead of time and, at times, travels many miles out of his way to avoid bridges.

The personal circumstances of Sarah and Azid, their ages or lifestyles, may be different from your own. However, the techniques that they have used to help them to overcome their phobias are the same as the ones that should help you. In Section 5, you can read their full stories and how they used CBT self-help to enable them to feel better. They discuss what went well and what they found to be more challenging, as well as how they overcame the difficulties that they encountered along the way. It may not always be easy for you either but reading about others' experiences can help you to keep on track.

Sarah's story

Sarah is a twenty-three-year-old single, full-time mother. She has always been fearful of spiders (her 'feeling' symptoms). If she saw a spider she immediately had to leave the room and ask someone to remove it for her (her 'behaviour' symptoms). She found it impossible to be near them. The erratic way that they move frightened her. She was worried about them jumping on her and thought that they were creepy and would get tangled in her hair (her 'thinking' symptoms). She knew that this fear was irrational and, on one level, knew that these creatures couldn't hurt her. However, this didn't seem to help to subdue her fear or allow her to gain full control of her life. When she saw a spider, her heart pounded, and she shook (her 'physical/ body' symptoms).

She remembers having had this fear in her childhood. She recalled a situation where a boy brought a spider into school in a jam jar. She remembers being absolutely terrified by it.

Certain situations were particularly worrying for her. She hated going into dusty dark areas where she thought that spiders tended to be. She could not go into her attic. Since she separated from her partner, Mike, if anything needed to be brought down from the attic she had to ask her father to do it. She also worried about walking in some natural areas where she believed that she would unwittingly walk through spiders' cobwebs and end up with a spider crawling on her. This limited some of the activities that she could do with her son. She worried that she wouldn't be comfortable taking him out into the countryside when he gets older.

The final straw came when there was a spider on his cot. She wasn't able to comfort him whilst he was crying. Sarah wanted to remove the spider, but she was unable to do so. She had to phone her father to help her. This worried her and made her feel as if she was failing as a mother. As a result, she went to see her family doctor, Dr Brown.

Sarah told Dr Brown about the overwhelming physical sensations that she experienced if she was near a spider. She also had an overwhelming urge to escape from any situation with a spider in it or avoid any situations where spiders might be present. She became quite tearful with Dr Brown when she spoke about the situation involving the cot. Dr Brown listened sympathetically and asked Sarah about what else was happening in her life. Sarah mentioned that things were now more stressful for her as a young single mother and life was more challenging since Mike left.

Dr Brown said that he felt that Sarah was experiencing a phobia. He could not say for sure what was causing it. It may be that it has always been there in the background. Sarah remembers being afraid of spiders as a child. He wondered whether her increasing stress and responsibilities, together with less support, meant that it was interfering more with her life now. He also said that reading a self-help book called *How to Beat Fears and Phobias One Step at a Time* should be helpful for her. He said that this book would give her more information about fears and it would take her through a CBT intervention called graded exposure therapy to help her to overcome these difficulties.

Sarah was a little sceptical about whether a book could help her. However, after she started to read the book, she soon realised that CBT self-help was one of the recommended treatments for her difficulties. Sarah also thought that this way of working would be really useful for her as she would be in control of her treatment and could more easily plan it around her other responsibilities. You can find out how Sarah responded to her treatment in Section 5.

Azid's story

Azid is forty-two years old and he has been a salesman for most of his working life.

He currently travels between professional kitchens selling kitchen equipment. Because he travels across the whole of the north of England, this means that he can spend a great deal of time driving. Azid remembers that in the past, his father was also generally worried about heights and was wary of driving over bridges.

Azid does not remember having this problem until about a year ago when he was driving over a tall bridge on a particularly windy day as he was going home. There were big digital traffic signs warning high-sided vehicles to be careful on the entry to the bridge. Azid was driving on the outermost lane of the dual carriageway over the bridge. As a lorry passed, the wind caught its trailer and it swerved in front of him. Azid braked quickly to avoid it and almost hit the side-barrier of the bridge. He was extremely shaken at the time but managed to continue driving and got home. When he arrived at home he ran the event over and over in his mind, believing that he could easily have driven over the side of the bridge (his 'thinking' symptoms). In his mind's eye, he saw himself falling from the bridge and his car hitting the water below.

When he next set off to the same destination he began to think about driving over the bridge. He experienced anxiety (his 'feeling' symptoms). His heart quickened, and he noticed that he was sweating and gripping the steering wheel more tightly (his 'physical/body' symptoms). He found himself re-routing himself to use the tunnel under the river rather than the bridge (his 'behaviour' symptoms). This meant that he needed to go out of his way and was also charged a toll to go through the tunnel. However, avoiding the bridge made him feel enormously relieved. He found himself avoiding this and other bridges in the future when driving his family around at weekends. He then found that whilst travelling on his own, his heart would pound, and he would feel very hot and sweaty when driving over other bridges as well. In time, he started to avoid these bridges too.

These changes to his route sometimes added an hour to his working day. Azid was arriving home later in the evenings after work. His wife asked him to see his doctor, Dr Chen, to see whether he could be helped to overcome his problem. Dr Chen recommended that Azid went to see his local IAPT/NHS service. Azid contacted the service and John, a PWP, arranged to call him for an initial screening appointment to discuss both his problem and any help that he might need. Azid was offered a choice of whether to have treatment by telephone support or go to a local community centre to see John. He arranged to see John on Friday afternoons as he was usually at the local sales office then and so could attend more easily. John spoke to Azid about the pattern that maintains his fear (as described in Section 2) and overviewed an achievable treatment approach to allow him to overcome his phobia (as described in Section 3).

Azid was attracted to this approach and felt that it was relevant to his problem. John explained that they would be using this book to guide the treatment together. Azid found this to be useful because it gave him the opportunity to overview the principles of treatment whenever he wanted, outside of the sessions. If he had any queries, experienced any hiccups or was uncertain about any aspect of the treatment, he knew that he would be able to 'bounce' these off John in the next session.

John explained that this CBT self-help book is written in a straightforward way. It would take Azid through the treatment step by step, and Azid would be in control of the pace of treatment at all times. The CBT technique used is called graded exposure therapy (we come to this in Section 3). The focus for this is overcoming fear in a structured and graded way. This technique should allow Azid to get back to the lifestyle that he enjoyed before this problem developed. See how Azid got on with CBT self-help in Section 5.

Questions and answers

Sarah and Azid's stories show how people can experience a phobia very differently. You may still have questions about fears or phobias, and why this has happened to you. Below, I will try to answer some of the most common questions people have about phobias.

Question 1: What is a phobia?

A phobia (in the scientific literature this is termed a 'specific phobia') is a disorder consisting of a marked and persistent anxiety or fear, caused by at least one object or situation. This interferes greatly with the person's lifestyle and/or results in a lot of distress. Strictly speaking, to meet the diagnosis, the person needs to have had the problem for at least six months. The distress includes symptoms such as:

- Fast heart rate and breathing

- Muscle tension, trembling

- Sweating

- Hotness or flushed skin

- A sharpening of the senses

The objects or situations that trigger the fear can be linked to:

- animals (for example, snakes, dogs, spiders, wasps, rats)

- situations (such as driving, flying, going to the dentist, escalators)

- the natural environment (for instance, heights, water, thunderstorms)

- other categories (such as clowns, foods, vomiting, choking)

Some useful information about specific phobias is available on the NHS website. At the time of writing, a direct link to the relevant webpage is: https://www.nhs.uk/conditions/phobias/.

The charity Mind also has some extensive information on their website and the direct link for this is:

https://www.mind.org.uk/information-support/
types-of-mental-health-problems/phobias/

Question 2: What causes fear and phobias?

Not everyone can pinpoint a cause for the development of their phobia. It may be due to a combination of factors rather than one alone. Here are some of the reasons why phobias can develop:

1. *Pre-programming.* To understand fear, we need to go back in time. It is believed that our earliest ancestors evolved some four to seven million years ago. Fossils of humans have been dated to approximately 200,000 years ago. However, the modern 'civilised' human (in other words, you and I) has only existed for a few thousand years. So, for most of our existence, the kinds of threats that we faced were not things such as 'I must hit my sales target today' or 'I need to find the money to pay for a new washing machine', but rather 'that wild animal could kill me' or 'those strangers may attack me and take away all of my food'.

   To help us deal with these primitive threats, our bodies developed a defensive system that we call the *fight or flight response*. When this is activated by a threat, our body goes into a kind of overdrive. We breathe more quickly and our heart pounds to make more energy available to our muscles. We go red and sweat because our body will need to work harder to keep cool because of the efforts it is likely to make. Our senses sharpen to allow us to be more vigilant to possible dangers. These changes are designed to help us fight or run away – so they are termed the fight or flight response. This reaction developed over time to help us to deal with the threats that existed in our environment over the vast duration of our evolution.

Some of the triggers to this response seem to be pre-programmed into our bodies. Toddlers may be fearful of things such as snakes, spiders and heights, even though they have not had any bad experiences linked to them. This makes sense as toddlers are so vulnerable. This pre-programming provides an extra layer of protection for them. These fears may help to stop them from falling or getting poisonous bites. Many more adults are fearful of spiders or snakes than electrical sockets or cars, even though these modern items are generally more dangerous. This also adds weight to the idea that we are pre-programmed to be wary of the primal threats that confronted pre-civilised man. We are more likely to develop a phobia linked to these pre-programmed things as we are more sensitive towards them.

2. *Observation.* We can also learn to be fearful of the things that we see. If we see someone step on a landmine, we learn to be fearful of that area and avoid it. If we are startled by a vicious dog guarding a property, we learn to be wary and cross the road as we approach the property to avoid being startled in the future.

3. *What we are taught.* Similarly, we learn to be fearful of the things that other people tell us are dangerous. As a child, if our parents tell us to avoid dogs because they can bite, or show us that they are fearful of them, this can fuel a fear of dogs. In this way, anxious parents can, without meaning to, contribute to the development of a phobia.

4. *Experience.* Fears can develop through 'conditioning'. This is a process where, when we are shocked by an object or situation in some way, we can become fearful of it. For instance, a fear of dogs may emerge after being bitten by one.

5. *Life changes and stresses.* Finally, in times of stress, when we can feel more threatened and anxious in our lives, we are generally more prone to developing symptoms. For example, if we have been away from work due to a

long-term illness, we can become quite anxious about returning.

Question 3: Why does having a phobia feel that it has taken over my life?

If you remember, in Section 1, I mentioned how avoidance may seem quite natural to you when it comes to the things that your phobia influences. This is because fears can grow and turn into phobias through a common vicious cycle involving avoidance.

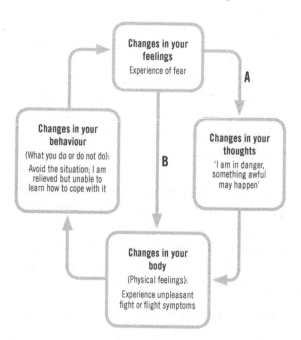

We heard earlier in this section that symptoms can each affect each other in complicated ways. Here is an example of how they can fit together to worsen fear and impair lifestyle. In response to fear, individuals can experience thoughts focused on threat ('that dog will bite me') which can then, in turn, trigger the unpleasant physical symptoms associated with the fight or flight response (such as sweating and heart pounding). This is path A in the diagram above. Alternatively, some people are more unaware of these thoughts and are more aware of the unpleasant physical symptoms (path B). In either case, the unpleasant symptoms can be taken to confirm the presence of threat ('because I am anxious I am in danger'), and people naturally avoid the thing that tends to trigger this experience (the dog). This provides a powerful sense of relief which, in psychological terms, is very rewarding. Additionally, avoidance robs the individual of opportunities to master more productive ways of coping with the fear. As such, things remain stuck. Imagine a situation where a child thinks that there is a monster under their bed. If they never lift up the bedspread to check, they won't discover that it is just their imagination! This is the source of the great power of the avoidance cycle: it denies individuals the opportunity to move forward.

Above and beyond this, once individuals start to

avoid, there is a natural process (termed 'general-isation') where things that share similar features with the original thing are avoided as well. So, if an individual originally avoids clowns, they might begin to avoid other costumed characters who wear make-up that remind them of clowns. If they avoid one dog, they may start to avoid other dogs as well. If they avoid one food because the texture makes them worry that it may cause them to choke, they may start to avoid other foods with a similar texture as well. In this way, fears can naturally grow through this cycle of avoidance and the process of generalisation. As they grow, they tend to interfere with more and more of an individual's lifestyle.

Question 4: Why me?

As you will have read above, it is often difficult to pinpoint a clear reason why this has happened to you. There is no simple explanation that can predict who will develop a phobia and who will not. What is clear is that phobias are common. They are the most common mental health issue in women and in men who are over twenty-five years old, with around 7 to 10 per cent of adults experiencing the condition over the period of a year. In other words, in a room of a hundred people, as many of ten of them will currently experience a phobia or will develop one in the near future. So, as you can see, it is not at all unusual to have a phobia. What is important is working out what keeps it going and how you can overcome it. This will help you both now and in the future should you ever begin to experience similar symptoms again. Working through this book and putting its techniques into action will help you to overcome your fear.

Question 5: What can be done to overcome fears and phobias?

The good news is that there is a psychological treatment available for your phobia. This has been extensively researched and is known to work for many of the people who use it. The approach is based upon a psychological therapy that I mentioned earlier. This is called CBT. This approach is very structured and practical, and so lends itself really well to a self-help format. As I also mentioned earlier, this format is referred to as low intensity CBT. This consists of using self-help materials with the same content and techniques that you would cover if you were seeing a therapist in face-to-face sessions. The approach can be used without any support from a trained health professional but having support can be really helpful for some people, especially those who might otherwise struggle to remain motivated. Many people make use of support through their doctor, practice nurse or, in IAPT/NHS, a PWP. I provided a link for you to find your local IAPT services earlier on page 21.

Question 6: Will it happen again?

I have more good news to offer you here. Of those who are treated for anxiety conditions, over 75 per cent remain well after two years of monitoring. However, the flip side of this is that others will experience anxiety symptoms again in the future. There is no agreed way of predicting who will relapse and who will not. However, we do know that people who are able to spot early warning signs that symptoms may be returning will do better. This awareness allows individuals to put the techniques that worked for them previously into practice to stop these early signs becoming a full-blown relapse (details of what a 'relapse' is are in Section 4). However, it needs to be borne in mind that we all experience fear and anxiety at times. This is a natural protective response to threat. So, it is really important not to misinterpret normal experiences as being a problem.

In Section 4 you will be introduced to a 'relapse prevention toolkit'. Should you begin to see the early warning signs of your phobia returning (for instance, if you start to have an urge to avoid some situations), you can use the toolkit to head off a relapse. Unfortunately, I cannot guarantee that you will not experience a return of your symptoms in the future. But the tools and techniques that you will learn in this book will better equip you to get on top of the issue again. These are lifelong skills to help you to keep on top of your phobia. Rather than try to avoid experiencing your phobia again, it is more helpful to keep an eye out for early warning signs that indicate to you (or others who are close to you) that issues may be returning.

How are your own fears or phobias affecting you?

So far, I have explored with you how fears and phobias:

- Are generally experienced emotionally.

- Can affect us physically.

- Can affect our thoughts.

- Affect what we do (or don't do) differently.

Now I would like to apply this understanding to your situation. Here is the example of how these symptoms relate to each other for Azid when he is confronted by situations related to driving and bridges:

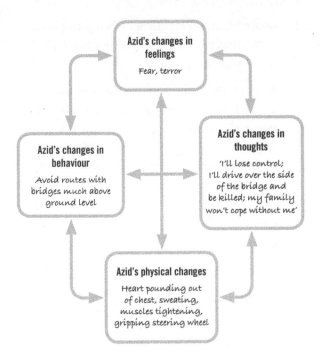

Using this example, fill in the areas of the diagram below which have space for you to list the symptoms triggered by the thing that you fear:

1. What is the *feeling* that you experience when you are confronted (or imagine that you are confronted) with your feared thing? Write that in the feelings box.

2. What *physical changes in your body* have you

noticed that you experience when your phobia is affecting you? Write these down in the physical changes box.

3. Next, think about how feeling this way has affected *what you are doing*. In the behaviour box, make a note of the things that you have stopped doing or are avoiding because of the phobia. Also think of the things that you may be doing extra (for example, drinking more alcohol or asking people to accompany you more).

4. Now consider whether you are aware of the kinds of *thoughts that go through your mind* when you are affected by your phobia. Add these into the thoughts box. These are likely to be focused on some form of threat. Don't worry if you are not aware of any thinking patterns: not everyone is.

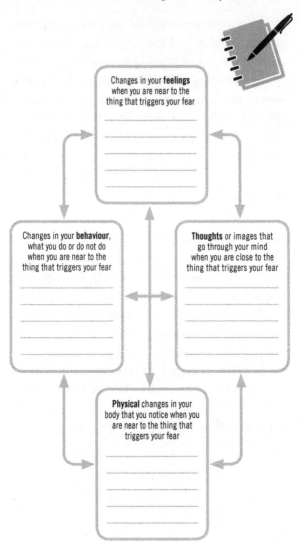

Changes in your **feelings**
when you are near to the
thing that triggers your fear

_____
_____
_____
_____

Changes in your **behaviour**,
what you do or do not do
when you are near to the
thing that triggers your fear

_____
_____
_____
_____

Thoughts or images that
go through your mind
when you are close to the
thing that triggers your fear

_____
_____
_____
_____

Physical changes in your
body that you notice when you
are near to the thing that
triggers your fear

_____
_____
_____
_____

As we saw earlier, when we were discussing how phobias develop and are maintained, these areas can interact and fuel each other. Breaking into this cycle by affecting one of these areas will stop and reverse the vicious cycle. In doing so, it should affect all of the other areas. This then turns into a new positive virtuous cycle (indicated in bold in the next diagram) as the treatment reduces symptoms and increases confidence. As you move around the virtuous cycle again and again, you are likely to feel better and better.

Just as it took time to develop your vicious cycle, it will take some time to reverse it and turn it into a virtuous one. I am here to show you the steps that you can take to allow this to happen. The biggest step is acknowledging that you really want to change. You have done that already. You have also thought about some goals for your treatment and when you are going to carry it out. You are now ready to move to Section 3 where we will look together at how you can break this cycle and begin to make the steps required to allow you to start to feel better.

GRADED EXPOSURE TREATMENT

If you have completed Sections 1 and 2, well done! I hope that you have found the information about fears and phobias to be really useful. Do you see aspects of your own problem reflected in both the theory and the case examples? I am really pleased that you have stayed with me so far and I hope that you are reassured that there is an evidence-based treatment for your phobia.

If your symptoms have a different pattern from those that I described in the last section, it may be that you have a different psychological problem. If this is the case, if you have not done so already, it would be worthwhile talking to your doctor before you continue any further. There are a variety of anxiety problems. Phobias are just one type of these.

If you have turned straight to this section because either you want to get going with your treatment straight away or you may know about phobias already, welcome aboard! By way of a brief recap, in the last section we spent time looking at the following:

- The factors that influence the development of phobias.

- The vicious cycle of avoidance that maintains a phobia.

- We also looked at your symptoms and goals in Section 1.

In terms of your own symptoms, you were able to compare them to the symptoms experienced by Sarah and Azid, our case examples. If you haven't completed this exercise, please turn back to page 57 and fill in your symptoms in the diagram as these will be your target for treatment through use of the techniques described in this section. It would be also helpful if you could have a look at the vicious cycle of avoidance (page 49). You may also want to complete your goals for treatment (pages 26–7). These will help you to focus in this section and will also allow you to monitor change over time.

Now it is time to break into the vicious cycle of avoidance that maintains your phobia and start to enter the virtuous one. In this section, we are going to work together to overcome your fear using graded exposure therapy (GET). This is an intervention that is a part of CBT (I described CBT early on page 5). Here, you will learn about GET and how it works. We will then make a plan to put GET into action.

Key points

Remember that you are in charge of your treatment. If you are not clear about anything, please feel free to reread the relevant parts of the book again. You can turn back and look at any of the notes that you have made in the margin or any of the text that you have highlighted – this should be helpful. If it is helpful, keep making notes and highlighting as you go on from this point. The key thing is to use this book to *apply* GET and put it into action to change your life. Reading the book alone without this action will not be enough to overcome your phobia.

What is GET?

In order to understand GET, we need to return to the nature of fears. We all have them and we all have had to overcome them at some point in our lives. What can we learn from this that we can apply to overcoming a phobia now? Now let's think about this briefly.

We overcome fear when we learn to swim. We naturally tend to have a fear of water because it can be life-threatening. It is very difficult to overcome this fear without actually being in water. We know this from the avoidance cycle, but we can probably also see this from a logical perspective as well.

Let's imagine that, as a child, we are in the pool for the first time. We are being supported by a parent in the shallow end near to the edge of the pool, whilst wearing inflatable arm bands. We are likely to be extremely anxious in this situation at first. The water is splashing our face and going into our mouth. We are extremely uncomfortable. We may struggle to breathe at times. The water may make our eyes sore. We may then scream and cry. What happens after a while as we become familiar with the situation? The anxiety begins to slowly settle. We can understand this from an evolutionary perspective. As we sense that the threat associated with a situation reduces, our body turns off the fight and flight response to conserve its energy. We can see this in pattern A of the graph below ('Exposure'). This process of anxiety reducing over time is called 'habituation'. If we remain in the situation, anxiety lessens. If we had avoided swimming pools altogether, this habituation would not have had an opportunity to occur and so the level of threat posed by the pool would remain the same.

Let's imagine that our parent took us into the pool for a few moments, we felt overwhelmed, screamed and shouted, and our parent then took us quickly out again because we were upset. When we calmed down, they had another go at taking us into the pool, but took us quickly out again after we screamed and shouted again, and so on. This is pattern B in the graph ('Avoidance'). On each entry to the pool, the level of anxiety is the same because we have not stayed in the pool long enough for habituation to occur. We may experience this process as a number of 'short, sharp shocks'. What is likely to happen to our fear in this scenario? It remains unchanged and may even worsen. In this way, the first principle of GET is that exposure to the fear must be *prolonged*.

If our parent took the 'Exposure' approach (situation A in the graph below), as we return to the pool in the future and under the same conditions (in the shallow end near the side, wearing arm bands whilst supported by a parent), our level of anxiety tends to lessen each time. (In GET, each time we expose ourselves to the feared thing, this is called a 'practice session'.) We get used to the pool and our confidence increases. This is shown in the second graph, found on page 67. The anxiety lessens *over*

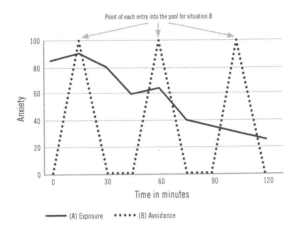

Point of each entry into the pool for situation B

——— (A) Exposure   • • • • (B) Avoidance

practice sessions 1 to 3 as well as *within* each session as well. So, the next principle of GET is that exposure should be regularly *repeated*.

Of course, at this point, we have not yet completely overcome our fear of water. We are just beginning to feel comfortable in the shallow end near to the edge of the pool, with arm bands and whilst supported by our parent. This is progress but it is just the start. What about the rest of the pool? What about being in the pool without our parent? We need to build up the challenge of the situation gradually to conquer these other aspects. In this way, as the anxiety for a situation reduces, when we feel ready, the challenge of the situation is then increased to another level or step. It might be that the next step is for our

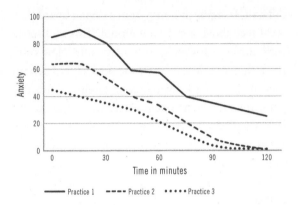

parent to take us away from the edge of the pool and stay with us there. We will feel more anxious. This is to be expected. We are further away from the safety of the side of the pool. The habituation process will then occur again in this new situation as we become familiar with it; and so on, step by step. This is the opposite of being thrown in the deep end. The feared thing is faced in a graded and controlled fashion consisting of several such steps of increasing challenge. This *graded* approach is the third principle of GET.

You may feel a little overwhelmed by the idea that you will be facing some challenging situations in due course. Don't worry. By the time you will be considering the more challenging objects or situations linked to your fear, they will seem less difficult. Imagine jumping from a diving board that is 20 feet above a swimming pool. This will seem very anxiety-provoking to most people. Now consider that you have, over time, gradually become used to jumping from increasing heights into the pool. You are now at a stage where you can comfortably jump into the pool from a board that is 15 feet above the water. The 20-foot board would now seem to be less intimating wouldn't it? This is also what we find as people work towards confronting things that are linked to their phobia. As they progress, the more challenging situations that they have yet to face become less intimidating for them.

Finally, let's consider another example. Imagine that you are somewhat fearful of riding roller coasters. You have been placed on one that is anxiety-provoking but just within your reach in terms of challenge. You are sitting in the coaster whilst blindfolded and have soundproof headphones on with music playing through them. In this way, you are cut off from some of your senses. You go around the circuit of the ride a few times. Now let's imagine that the blindfold and headphones are taken off as you are mid-ride on the coaster. For the first time, you experience it in its full glory (or horror!). You experience the height, see the speed and now fully hear the screams of the other passengers. Will your fear now go up or down? It probably will go up because you are now experiencing the full magnitude of the experience. Distractions, which draw away our attention, reduce the magnitude of the experience and, in so doing, do not allow the process of habituation to fully occur. For this reason, the final condition of GET is that exposure should occur *without distraction*. In other words, you should direct your attention towards, and remain as fully focused as possible upon, the feared thing throughout the practice session.

Incidentally, the reason why it is advised that some medications for psychological problems (or other substances such as alcohol) are not used at the same time as GET is that they can also interfere with this habituation process. Consequently, when you reduce the dose of a particular medication, the level of anxiety can rise again.

> To reduce fear, exposure within GET should be:
>
> - Prolonged
> - Repeated
> - Graded
> - Without distraction

Applying GET

Health professionals have used these principles, which allow us to overcome fear naturally, to apply GET to overcome phobias. It may be that just the thought of using a form of exposure to overcome your phobia may be making you anxious at this point. Don't worry. GET is particularly structured to make this process manageable for you.

Key features of GET

- Helps people identify the things that trigger their fear.

- Provides a structured approach that enables people to face fear in a controlled manner.

- Helps find a manageable starting point for the therapy by grading the feared situations or objects from least to most feared.

- Enables the breaking of the avoidance cycle and habituation.

- Allows increasingly feared objects or situations to be conquered in a controlled manner through the use of a 'ladder' of increasingly challenging situations.

- Allows individuals to reclaim their lifestyle as fear reduces or disappears.

Applying GET entails four stages and I will now work through each of these in turn with you.

Stages of GET

- Stage 1: Identify feared thing(s).

- Stage 2: Grade these to create an exposure ladder.

- Stage 3: Set up conditions for habituation.

- Stage 4: Work your way up the ladder.

Stage 1: Identify feared thing(s)

Feared things are objects or situations that are avoided or, at times, experienced with discomfort or distress. These often centre around a theme which defines the phobia (for instance, a fear of dogs or a fear of escalators). These will usually be relevant to the goals that you listed on pages 28–31. Overcoming your fear is likely to be either a part of your goals or should help you to achieve these goals. Overcoming a fear of escalators helps to achieve a goal 'to be able to feel comfortable moving around in any shopping centre'. Overcoming a fear of dogs helps to achieve a goal of 'being able to visit my friends who have dogs at their homes'.

Here are some questions that will help you to pinpoint your feared things:

•   In what way is your phobia interfering with your life?

•   What situations or objects are you fearful of?

•   Are there any situations or objects that you would like to stop avoiding?

•   What have you stopped doing now, that you used to do before your phobia developed?

Sarah's feared things

Spiders

Attics

Garages, sheds and workshops

Dusty old houses

Walking through bushes and high plants that are close together

Spider sections of zoos

Now take a moment to make a list of your feared things.

Your feared things

....

....

....

....

....

....

....

....

....

Even though individuals may be fearful in a situation, some factors may make it either easier or more difficult for them to tolerate it. For example, someone who is afraid of dogs may be more fearful of larger dogs, livelier dogs or dogs not on leads. A person fearful of escalators may find smaller ones easier or may find it easier to go up than down them. Let's now try to think of all the varieties of situations that are relevant to the thing that you fear. What would make it easier or more difficult for you? Here are some questions that should help you to pinpoint this:

- What sort of things do you do that you find help to reduce the level of fear?

- Is there anything about the thing that would make it more or less intense for you?

- Would the situation differ if you were near or close to the thing?

- Would the time of day have any impact on your level of discomfort?

What affects Sarah's level of anxiety that is associated with her feared thing

Size of spider

If spider is living or dead

If spider is real or a toy

If spider is really present or if it is a picture/video of a spider

If I can see cobwebs in rooms, attics or between bushes or plants

If someone is with me for support

What affects your level of anxiety that is associated with your feared thing

....

....

....

....

....

....

....

....

....

Now you should have pinpointed your feared thing, and you will also have a list of situations or influences that affect the amount of fear you experience when in the presence of your feared thing.

Stage 2: Grade these to create an exposure ladder

We are now halfway through the planning stage of your treatment. Our next step is to create an exposure 'ladder' out of the situations that you have described in the last two exercises. A ladder is a list of situations that involve exposing yourself to your feared thing, in order of increasing challenge. The easiest is the bottom rung of the ladder and the most difficult is at the top.

Creating a ladder

- Combine the list of feared things you produced earlier with the situations that make them easier or more difficult, to produce a much longer list.

- Rank all of the things on the list on a scale of 0–100, zero being that you predict that it would produce no anxiety at all, 100 being that you would become as anxious as you could imagine.

- Place these in the order of your ratings of anxiety, lowest at the bottom, highest at the top.

- Now pick eight to twelve of these to focus on that are fairly equally spaced along the 0–100 scale. These should be practical to arrange within an exposure session. For example, Sarah may have put a particular type of spider on her list (such as tarantula) but has no means of getting access to one. So, there is little point in including this on her ladder.

- Only include things that you can't do due to your level of fear or that you are avoiding at the moment. This may mean that you only include those situations rated 30/100 or higher because if they create less anxiety than this, you may be already doing them.

- Place these on the exposure ladder worksheet provided on page 82.

Let's have a look at Sarah and Azid's ladders before you construct your own. (Details of the bridges mentioned are available at www.bridgesonthetyne.co.uk.)

Once you've looked at Sarah and Azid's ladders you can complete your own (on page 82) by placing each situation involving your feared thing on a step of the ladder. If you find that your feared things revolve around more than one theme or phobia (for example, a fear associated with dogs and heights), pick the one that is interfering with your life the most and just focus on that. You can repeat the whole process at a later point for another phobia that is troubling you.

Sarah's ladder

LEVEL OF ANXIETY	SITUATION/OBJECT CAUSING FEAR	ANXIETY RATING (0-100)
	Spend time in the attic	100
	Spider crawls on my bare arm	90
	Spider crawls on my sleeve	80
	Spider crawls on my trouser leg	75
Most anxiety	Spider crawls on my shoe whilst I'm wearing it	65
	Spider crawls on desk whilst I'm on my own	65

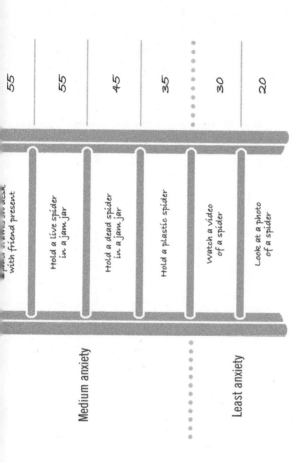

55

55

45

35

30

20

...with friend present

Hold a live spider
in a jam jar

Hold a dead spider
in a jam jar

Hold a plastic spider

Watch a video
of a spider

Look at a photo
of a spider

Medium anxiety

Least anxiety

Azid's ladder

LEVEL OF ANXIETY	SITUATION/OBJECT CAUSING FEAR	ANXIETY RATING (0-100)
	Drive over Redheugh Bridge (very high, low sides, road close to edge), outer lane, children in car	100
	Drive over Redheugh Bridge (very high, low sides, road close to edge), outer lane, on my own	95
	Drive over Redheugh Bridge (very high, low sides, road close to edge), inner lane, on my own	85
Most anxiety	Drive over Tyne Bridge (high, more enclosed), outer lane, on my own	85
	Drive over Tyne Bridge (high, more enclosed), inner lane, on my own	80
	Drive over Scotswood Bridge (medium high), outer lane, on my own	75

(medium high), inner lane, on my own — 70

Passenger in car driving over Redheugh Bridge (very high, low sides, road close to edge), outer lane — 60

Passenger in car driving over Tyne Bridge (high, more enclosed), outer lane — 50

Medium anxiety.

Drive over Swing Bridge, (very low, small), on my own — 50

Drive over Swing Bridge, (very low, small), with partner in passenger seat — 45

Least anxiety

Watch video of driving over bridges, seen from driver's viewpoint — 15

Your ladder

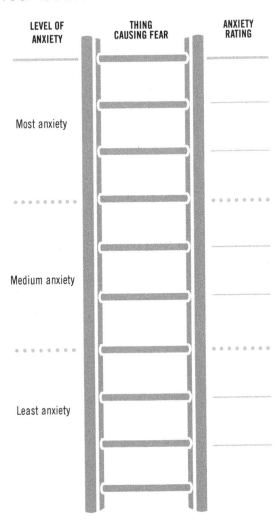

Well done! You have now completed most of the planning linked to GET.

Stage 3: Set up conditions for habituation

Now we are going to use all of the hard work you've done in Stages 1 and 2 in this section to construct your first 'practice session'. This is a situation that is constructed in a way that will allow habituation to happen to one of the feared things that you have placed on the steps of your ladder. We are going to plan how you are going to begin to face your fear in a way that you are in control and at a pace that is acceptable to you. You may have tried to face your fears several times before. However, this time we are going to use the principles listed on page 69. Can you remember what these are? In a moment or two we will apply these principles to your treatment.

Let's think about where to start on your ladder. We want to pick a rung that is challenging, but not completely overwhelming. We want you to be sure that you can both succeed in your first practice session *and* experience the habituation process. Quite frequently, people can imagine starting with a practice session that they predict will result in around 50/100 on their scale of anxiety. If you sense that this is too much for you to make a start, think about a lower rung. Now we will plan a practice session that is based upon this rung of the ladder.

Let's think of the practicalities involved in your first practice session. Here are some useful questions that Sarah considered before her first session (which involved holding a dead spider in a jam jar), that you can adapt for your own use:

- When am I going to do the first practice session?

  (Try to start your practice sessions as soon as possible. Procrastination can make starting GET more difficult.)

- Who will be bringing the dead spider in a jam jar to the house?

- How will this be arranged with them?

- Will they be able to come back to take the dead spider away or can I keep it somewhere myself (like the garden shed)?

- If I need them to bring over a spider, will they be available at other points in the week as well, so this can be repeated a number of times?

- What would it be helpful to tell this person about my phobia and will they be supportive?

You now have a date and a time for your first practice session, and you also have thought through in Section 1 how you are going to dedicate time to GET. Remember that the exposure session should be *prolonged* so you should plan to have enough time for habituation to occur. I would suggest that you allow ninety minutes for this initially. To allow habituation to occur, you should stay in the situation until your level of anxiety *has reduced by 50 per cent*. So, if your level was 50/100 initially, stay in the situation until it is 25/100 or lower. The length of your practice session is determined by the time it takes to achieve this 50 per cent reduction, *not by the duration of the time alone*.

Constructing practice sessions can require some creativity and support from others. To allow his practice sessions to extend to the required length of time, Azid had to drive repeatedly over the bridge in question – turning around and driving back over the bridge, turning around again, and so on – for the whole session until his 50 per cent reduction occurred. When Sarah moved on to working with a live spider, until she was able to capture a spider and release it herself, she needed a friend to scoop up the spider and place it in the correct situation for her exposure tasks.

Another condition for GET is that exposure in the practice session should occur *without distraction*. This means that you should ideally not be doing things in the session like: playing on a smartphone, listening to music, seeking reassurance, closing your eyes or only doing exposure tasks with another person present. Some people do find themselves needing to do some of these distracting activities initially to help them to cope with a situation. If this is the case with you that's fine, but plan a future step on the ladder that involves an exposure session where the same situation is confronted without doing the distracting activity.

One of Sarah's steps involved holding a jam jar with a live spider in it. Before the start of the session, she went to the toilet, turned off the television and put her smartphone out of reach and on 'silent mode'. The house was in silence. She arranged for her friend to bring the spider over in the jam jar with some air holes in the lid, at a specified time. She also arranged for her father to look after her son so that nothing would take her attention away from the task. She planned to do the practice session at the kitchen table with her back to the window, so she wouldn't be distracted by events outside.

After her friend had left, for the practice session itself, Sarah focused her attention on the spider as best as she was able for the entire time. She tried to let her eyes explore every part of it. She turned the jar in her hand to help with this. Initially, she could only hold it at arm's length, but as she settled she could hold it closer. She looked at how the light shone on the spider and how different parts of its body had different textures. She tried to see its eyes and its mouth. She noticed the patterns on its back and legs. She looked at it intensely as if she were going to draw it. She observed how it moved around the jar. She listened to hear if it made any sound against the glass. Whilst she was very anxious at first, she tried as best as she was able to focus her senses completely on the spider. This is really important as it enables habituation to occur, whereas if Sarah had distracted herself (for example, held the jar but looked at something else in the room) it is likely that she wouldn't have habituated to her anxiety.

Now you are ready to start your practice session. It is time to overcome your fear and start the virtuous cycle. It is really helpful to complete some ratings of your anxiety over this experience so that you can measure progress and so you know when you can leave the situation. *Rate your level of anxiety every five or ten minutes* on a piece of paper using a clock or a timer as a prompt, but record the following on the 'facing your fears rating sheet':

1. Both your level of anxiety and the time at the start of the practice session.
2. Your level of anxiety at its highest point.
3. Both the time and your level of anxiety at the end of the session (your anxiety level should have dropped by at least 50 per cent).
4. From the times recorded in 1) and 3), you can calculate the duration of the session, which goes in the final column. This duration should help with the planning of future sessions.

Facing your fears record sheet

Exposure task	Details of your feared thing for this session:

Date and time of planned practice sessions		Exposure anxiety ratings (0–100)			
		Start of session	Highest level	End of session	Duration of session
	Session 1				

Session 2	Session 3	Session 4	Session 5	Session 6	Session 7	Session 8

Another principle linked to GET is that exposure should be repeated. You will see that there is space on the record sheet above for quite a few practice sessions. You should undertake a practice session once a day for *at least* three to five days per week, but ideally daily. The more frequently you do the practice sessions, the quicker the progress you should make. If you are unable to do practice sessions frequently enough, fear can creep back over the period in between the sessions and so this will place a limit on the progress that you can make.

The success of GET can be strengthened by introducing variation into the practice sessions. For example, Sarah looked at different types of dead spider in a jam jar, rather than the same one for each session. Azid drove over a variety of bridges with a similar level of challenge for each step of his ladder rather than rigidly just sticking with the same bridge, even though that was the one that was named on that step of the ladder.

Stage 4: Climb the ladder

Begin treatment as soon as possible after you have constructed your ladder. Procrastination is a form of avoidance and so feeds into the vicious avoidance cycle. Start the practice sessions which are linked to the first step of the ladder that you are attempting (remember that this doesn't have to be the bottom step). If you are able to follow the principles of GET, you should notice that the level of anxiety that you experience at the start of the practice session gradually decreases, session by session, over time. You are slowly allowing the fight and flight response to reset itself for this particular situation. How quickly this occurs will vary according to the individual and the situation in question. But when you feel ready, you can then begin to move up and start the practice sessions that are linked to the next step up the ladder. As a rough guide, once your anxiety for a particular step has reduced to 20/100, providing that your steps on the ladder are fairly evenly spaced, there is a good chance that you will be more than ready to move up to the next step on the ladder. As you face situations, you may find that your level of anxiety differs from that which you predicted. In such instances, feel free to re-order the steps on your ladder as needed as you progress through your treatment.

Start a new worksheet for each step. There are more blank work sheets provided in the Further resources section at the back of this book. If you carry out more than eight practice sessions for a particular step, you will need to start a second worksheet for that same step.

Key point

Remember always to follow the principles of GET when planning and completing your practice sessions. Continue to complete the worksheets. Most people say that this really helps them, and you can look back over your worksheets to see the progress that you have made. This should increase your confidence and encourage you to keep moving forward.

The process is repeated until you have achieved the goals that you listed on pages 28–31. You should be more able to meet these goals as your levels of fear decrease. When you are able to achieve all of the steps on your ladder that impact upon your life, this is a natural place to end the treatment. This means that your fears are no longer significantly interfering with your lifestyle and you no longer have a phobia.

I mentioned earlier that you are bound to experience some hiccups along the way. In this final part of Section 3 we will look at some of the ways that these hiccups can be overcome.

Troubleshooting

Hopefully, GET has gone well for you and you haven't had to face any problems. Just in case you have, here are some ideas that may help you.

I am unable to construct a practice session that involves my particular phobia. Practice sessions are difficult to arrange for some types of fear, such as of thunderstorms or flying. In such instances, we can use a mix of both real aspects of the experience (such as the audio recordings of thunderstorms or a plane taking off) and our vivid imagination to construct a practice session. We call this type of practice session 'imaginary exposure'. For example, Julie had a fear of thunderstorms. For one of her practice sessions she found a smartphone insomnia app that included the sound of rain and thunderstorms that were intended to help people sleep. She purchased the app and played the sound loudly through her home audio system using the audio jack on her phone. She closed the curtains, closed her eyes and imagined as vividly as she could that she was in her garden under her gazebo whilst a thunderstorm was occurring all around her. She imagined that the rain was falling heavily. The plants and grass were wet. She pictured the flashes of lightning through the rain as the thunder sounded. Different forms of lightning were occurring in her mind, some far away and lighting up the clouds, some nearby that she could see directly. Doing imaginary exposure allowed Julie to build up to sitting out under her gazebo in a storm in real life.

If this is too difficult, it may be helpful for you to see a CBT therapist who can guide you through an imaginary exposure practice session and audio record it for you to then replay at home. I provided a link for you to find a local CBT therapist earlier on page 21.

Other options for imaginary exposure include virtual reality smartphone apps. You can place some smartphones into a kind of visor and wear connected headphones so that the app completely immerses you in a virtual experience. The apps, that are specifically designed to help people with phobias, then present you with scenes that can be placed on the different steps of your ladder (for instance, of thunderstorms of varying intensities). These apps are usually available through the app store for your smartphone.

I am unable to finish the practice session, I am too frightened. Sometimes people underestimate how much discomfort they will experience during a practice session and so are unable to complete it. Don't worry if this has happened to you. Here are some possible solutions:

- Adopt a coping strategy that will help you for this step, which can then be dropped in the future. One example of this is having someone with you during the practice session. Azid adopted this approach on the intermediate stage of his ladder. Perhaps you could use a form of distraction to reduce the intensity of the experience and then drop this in a later practice session?

- Construct an intermediate step on the ladder that is lower than the one you are attempting but still higher than the one that you have completed.

- Attempt the task using imaginary exposure during practice sessions first, before then returning to it in real life.

I stay in the practice session, but habituation doesn't occur, and my anxiety doesn't reduce by 50 per cent. Here are some possible solutions for this issue:

- Increase the length of the practice session. I suggested that you initially allow ninety minutes for this, but for some individuals habituation can take longer.

- Once again, you can construct a step on the ladder that is lower than the one you are attempting but still higher than the one that you have completed.

- Check that you are not taking any medication or using any other substances (such as alcohol or recreational drugs) that might interfere with the habituation process. Your doctor will be able to advise you about this.

My anxiety reduces *within* the practice sessions but does not go down *between* the practice sessions, so my peak anxiety remains quite similar for each session. Sometimes individuals who also experience depression display this pattern. If this is the case for you, seek treatment for your depression first and then come back to GET later.

I want to do the treatment, but other things are getting in the way. Reread the 'making change happen' part of Section 1 before returning to Section 3 when you are ready. Perhaps the time is not right for you at the moment to do GET? If so, don't worry. Come back to the treatment when you have more space in your life.

THE RELAPSE PREVENTION TOOLKIT

This section is for those who have already read the previous sections and have successfully completed their GET treatment. I hope that you are now in a virtuous cycle and are making progress towards meeting the goals that you made at the start of this journey (we'll revisit these later). Through your own hard work, you have successfully helped yourself to feel better. Now we need to keep an eye on this and check that you don't slip back into the vicious cycle of avoidance again. This is the final stage of the treatment – staying well and dealing with any difficulties that you may encounter in the future. To increase the chances of you staying well and keeping in the virtuous cycle, I would like to encourage you to work through this section. If you train hard and get fit through working out at a gym, isn't it important to continue some training to maintain your fitness? The same is the case with this psychological treatment. This is what we will be discussing next.

You may worry that you will lose some of the progress that you have made or worry about developing your phobia again in the future (this is called a
'relapse'). After they get well, people have questions
such as:

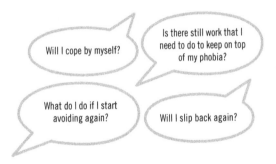

Once you begin to feel better, understandably you
want to maintain the positive changes that you have
achieved through your hard work. It can be fright-
ening to think that you might slip back and become
limited by fear once again.

If a health professional has supported your efforts
through the use of this book, being discharged from
their care may also produce concerns for you about
whether you can now continue to cope alone. A key
thing to remember is that it wasn't the support from
the professional that resulted in the habituation
process. Rather, it was the result of the hard work
that *you* put into the practice sessions. It was *your*

application of the knowledge and techniques that *you* have learned in this book that produced your recovery. You can successfully apply these techniques in the future if you need to. The use of this toolkit will help you to keep on track.

When someone has got on top of their fears, it is understandable that they do not wish for them to return again. This can mean that they begin to look out for any signs and symptoms that they are returning. They may misinterpret how they are feeling as an indication that they are slipping into a relapse. However, as I mentioned in Section 2, it is normal for us all to experience fear and anxiety at times. This is our body's natural defensive system. We cannot turn this off or cut it out! We can expect to experience anxiety symptoms more frequently or intensely if we have ongoing pressures in our lives, or if we are about to do something stressful, for example attending an interview or coping with a family member who is seriously ill. In such times, you may begin to avoid things again that were related to your phobia. This is termed a 'lapse' – a temporary return of symptoms. You may then worry that you are going to 'relapse' and your problem will return again.

What's the difference between a lapse and a relapse?

A *lapse* is a brief return to feeling more fearful or avoiding situations again in a way that might interfere with your life. Lapses are normal and occur occasionally. So long as you put into practice the principles of GET, you can get quickly back on track again. A lapse can become a relapse if you allow it to take hold. You may begin to feel hopeless about things which will worsen matters. Try to be patient and compassionate with yourself. See a lapse for what it is: just a temporary 'blip'. Try not to let it undermine your confidence by thinking of the worst-case scenario. If you do think negatively in this way, it may mean that you then switch into the vicious cycle of avoidance again (see the diagram below). Try not to avoid. If at all possible, try to keep doing all of the things that you have managed to achieve on your ladder. If some of the rungs have become a little more difficult, reapply GET to build up your confidence again. This will prevent a lapse from becoming a relapse. Don't give up. You know what works for you. Reapply these techniques and they will help you again.

A *relapse* is when fear and avoidance return over a longer period. The vicious cycle starts to spiral downward. The phobia 'takes hold' and begins to interfere significantly with your lifestyle once again. Here again, you have the knowledge and skills to reapply GET and recover. You know the principles of GET and how the treatment works. The task of recovery is easier if you catch matters sooner, before bad habits become ingrained into your lifestyle again. This is the reason why it is really helpful to learn to notice the early warning signs (or 'red flags') that indicate that things may be slipping backwards.

Important: Lapses may occur. Be realistic: you are likely to experience them at times. Recognise them for what they are and not as a sign that you have gone back to square one.

You have the tools to prevent a lapse from becoming a relapse. You know the function of the symptoms. You know how to overcome your fear if it persists. Don't imagine a 'doomsday' scenario where all of your problems are flooding back. In the diagram below, the box in bold indicates an experience of fear which may be encountered. Following this there are two 'forks in the road' indicated by the bold dotted lines/arrows. Remember that the virtuous cycle is the outside one and the vicious cycle is on the inside. According to which fork you take, you stay in the virtuous cycle or slip back into the vicious cycle. You will tend to remain in the virtuous cycle by:

- Keeping things in proportion and keeping in mind that you have the tools to overcome any issues if need be.

- Maintaining a pattern of behaviour where you are generally approaching things relating to your old phobia rather than starting to avoid them again.

If you feel the need, you can go back through Section 3 and reapply the techniques. This may increase your confidence and help you to get on top of your fears before things build up and possibly develop into a phobia again.

Hopefully, you will have learned from using this self-help book that techniques are available to help you to help yourself. Also, these can continue to be put into action in the future if you feel the need to do so. Making a relapse prevention plan and putting it into action when needed reduces the likelihood that you will slip back and that your phobia will return. It will also ensure that you have the confidence

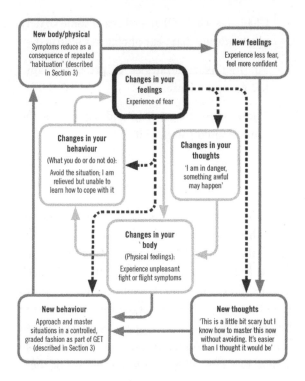

to spot any early warning signs or 'red flags'. This insight will then allow you to get on top of any symptoms as they occur.

You can think of this section as a toolkit to help you:

- Recognise the red flag situations that might lead you to start to avoid again.

- Challenge a belief that a return of some anxiety must indicate that your phobia has returned.

- Put into place strategies to prevent a lapse becoming a relapse.

- Know where to get help and support in the future should you need it.

My early warning signs

The first step in thinking about the future and dealing with any setbacks is to make a mental note of the things that you might notice when your fear begins to take hold. You may want to put this to the back of your mind. However, I would encourage you to spend some time thinking about this. These are the things that may indicate that issues are starting to come back in the future. If you notice them and take action, this may allow you to get on top of them before they begin to take hold and have an impact upon your life.

The diagram below will help you. In the diagram, write down the things that you think you may experience that are the first signs of problems happening. Think back to a time when your phobia was first developing. Write down the changes that you noticed in the following:

- Your *feelings*.

- Your *behaviour* (what you did more or less of).

- The *physical feelings* in your *body*.

- The patterns in your *thinking*.

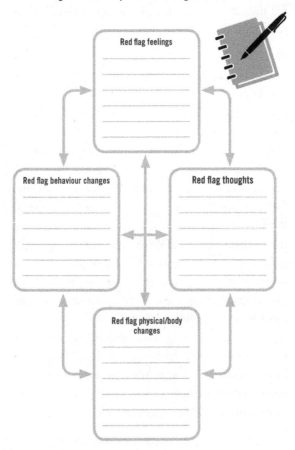

Red flags that I noticed when I first experienced my phobia

To help you to complete this diagram, you may want to turn back to the similar one that you completed on page 57. Think back to the time when you first felt unwell, prior to the point when you decided to seek help.

You could speak to someone who knew you well over this period of time when problems were developing, to get some clues. Often, other people can start to see change before we sense it ourselves. They can have some really helpful observations. Perhaps they noticed that you were starting to avoid some activities? It might be that you were doing more negative things to help you to cope (for instance, using alcohol or distracting techniques). It may be that you needed assistance for some things that you used to do on your own. They might remember you saying that you think that you can't do some things or making excuses not to do them (for example, with a fear of flying choosing to stay more local for holidays). Perhaps they noticed that you were experiencing some physical symptoms in your body in certain situations? It might be that you began to say more frequently that you were experiencing emotions such as fear. Perhaps you became more tense or irritable generally?

My red flags

My early warning signs are:

....

....

....

....

....

....

....

....

....

....

....

....

....

....

If you feel comfortable to do so, share your relapse plan with someone with whom you share your life. If you or your loved one notice that the red flags are creeping back into your life, now is a good time to take action. Use GET in the same way that you did before. If you have caught matters before they have slipped back too far, it should be more straightforward to regain the progress that you previously made.

Azid's partner noticed that he had started to avoid driving over the (high) Redheugh Bridge on windier days, preferring to take the tunnel under the river instead. After his partner pointed this out to Azid, he realised that he was slipping back into an avoidance cycle. In the evening after work on the next windy day, Azid undertook a practice session until habituation occurred. He repeated sessions on future windy days until the highest level of his anxiety over the practice sessions was reduced to 20/100. He then made a point of using the bridge on windy days in the future to maintain his confidence.

How things have improved since the start of treatment

Reflecting on what you have achieved is also an important part of relapse prevention. In the box below, list some of the improvements that you have noticed since starting treatment. These might be linked to your symptoms (feelings, behaviour, thoughts and body/physical), and also your lifestyle. Aspects of your lifestyle that might have changed include your:

- Relationships and social life (with partner, family, work colleagues and friends).

- Work life or ability to do other meaningful activity, such as voluntary work or being a carer for others.

- Ability to do essential things around the house such as housework, cleaning or DIY.

- Hobbies (solo ones such as model building or jigsaws, as well as ones with others such as sports or dancing).

In the boxes below, identify any positive improvements in these things:

Symptoms
Relationships and social life
Work or other meaningful activity

Essential things such as household responsibilities

Hobbies

Rerating your goals

In Section 1, I asked you to set some goals for yourself. You can now rerate them either by returning to the form that you used in Section 1 or by using the worksheet below. However you choose to complete the task, review the progress that you have made by comparing for each of them the first ratings of your goals to how you rate them now. Sometimes, when change happens steadily, week-by-week, it is easy to lose track of all the progress that you have made since the very start of the treatment, so this should help you to get a good sense of how much progress you have made.

My goals for feeling better

Goal 1: ....

....

.............................Today's date___/___/___

I can do this now (end of treatment rating; circle a number):

0	1	2	3	4	5	6
Not at all		Occasionally		Often		Any time

Goal 2: ....

....

....Today's date___/___/___

I can do this now (end of treatment rating;
circle a number):

0	1	2	3	4	5	6
Not at all		Occasionally		Often		Any time

Goal 3: ....

....

....Today's date___/___/___

I can do this now (end of treatment rating;
circle a number):

0	1	2	3	4	5	6
Not at all		Occasionally		Often		Any time

Take a moment to reflect on how far you have come!
Perhaps there are other things that have changed that

I have not asked you about? Perhaps you feel *happier* now that you have got on top of your problems?

What helped things to improve?

Which treatment techniques or strategies were particularly helpful in overcoming your fears? If you were able to go back in time and offer yourself some advice at the point when you were just starting the treatment, what advice would that be? For example, perhaps you might instruct yourself to be patient within the practice sessions or to make sure that you allow sufficient time? Perhaps you might say that it is important generally to approach rather than avoid? Make a note of this advice.

General advice

....

....

....

....

....

Now think about what advice you might give yourself if you became aware of a red flag situation which could result in a lapse. Perhaps the advice might be quite similar to that which you have just noted above? Alternatively, it might be completely different. For example, you might say that it is important to review your ratings on your 'ladder' once again and reinstate practice sessions as soon as you become aware of the lapse.

Advice in case of a red flag or lapse

....

....

....

....

....

The wellbeing review

The other really helpful strategy that I recommend is that you schedule a regular wellbeing review. Get a pen and paper and mark a day on your calendar each month. Alternatively, make a recurring entry in the electronic calendar on your smartphone that prompts you to undertake a wellbeing review. Having a review day will help you to spot red flags sooner and ensure that you keep on top of the techniques that we have covered together. Below is a structure to think through during your wellbeing review. It should take around twenty to thirty minutes. It is an opportunity to stop, think and reflect on how you are doing, and make any necessary 'course corrections'.

If you are seeing a health professional to support you through this treatment, it is likely that they will carry out at least one wellbeing review with you after you have finished treatment.

My wellbeing review

Review date:

What have my symptoms been like over the last month?

Reading through my red flags list, have I had any experiences that have concerned me?

Do I need to take any action now to keep on top of my fear?

If so, what will be helpful to use in my toolkit?

What do I need to do and when am I going to do it?

The date of my next review is:

Is there anything else that you would like to work on?

Remember I said in Section 3 that if you have any other fears or phobias that you want to work on, it is best to leave that until you have treated the phobia that is troubling you the most? There may be alternative things that you want to work on in the future. Some of your goals may not be completely met as yet. Are there any difficulties that are getting in the way of those? I would like to suggest that it is worth noting these down. This is so that you can remember them for later.

For the moment, it is best that you simply focus on maintaining the progress that you have made in regard to your current phobia. Once you have found that you have maintained progress for a few months, then you can return to this list. Depending on what problems remain, it may be that you can either apply GET to allow you to make progress or use another book from the How to Beat series. The other books are structured very similarly to this one but contain different treatment strategies for different issues. If you have managed to use this book, you should cope very well with the others in the series.

If you are being supported by a health professional, they should be able to help you to decide on how to move forward.

Issue(s) to work on in the future

What do you still want to work on?

At this point, do you have any ideas how you will do this?

When do you plan to do it (perhaps add in a reminder on your calendar for six months' time)?

Are there any resources that you need to get hold of to help with this?

Are there any things that might get in the way of you working on this, and how might you overcome these?

Relapse prevention top tips

Here are some top tips that may help you to use your toolkit to stay well:

1. The best way to prevent a lapse is to keep applying your GET skills to maintain confidence. Remember the fitness/gym example? Just because you get in shape does not mean to say that you should stop training. Perhaps, every so often, try to do new things that create a little

anxiety. Use the principles of GET to get on top of this anxiety if you need to. Perhaps you can learn to ice skate? Perhaps you can take an evening class at the local school or join a book club? Chose an activity that you can stay in for a while to allow habituation to occur.

2. Know your red flags. Watch out for times when you feel more stressed or when there is a lot of change in your life. Perhaps a relationship has ended, or you might be moving house? If you have shared your red flags with others, they may be able to notice early negative changes in your symptoms.

3. Complete a wellbeing review even if you have been feeling well. It will remind you to keep going with what has been successful.

4. Check that you haven't crept back into the negative avoidance cycle in any aspect of your life. If so, think about how you can apply GET to get back into a virtuous cycle where you are approaching things again.

5. Try not to be self-critical. Everyone is likely to experience a lapse at times. These are the body's natural response to situations that might be threatening. Focus on how you might stop a lapse from becoming a relapse.

6. The thought of having to focus on using the GET techniques again after you have completed treatment may be a little disheartening. Try rather to focus on how effective they were for you before in reducing your symptoms. If they worked for you previously, they are likely to work for you again.

7. Use your toolkit as often as you need to and remember to carry out your wellbeing reviews. These don't have to be monthly. You may want to make them weekly or fortnightly to start with. When you feel more confident in maintaining your progress, you can then space the reviews out again.

Getting further help if you need it

Sometimes, despite working as hard as you can and putting everything in place, you may still feel that you require additional help. Knowing where and how to get help is an important final component of your toolkit. I have listed some organisations that may be able to support you in the Further resources section at the back of the book, alongside spare copies of the additional worksheets that you will need for treatment. However, let's have a think about some of the people around you who can form part of your 'wellbeing team'.

Think of those around you who you trust and who could support you. Could you share your toolkit with them so that they can help you to watch out for any red flags? Having read your toolkit, they will also be aware of what you might need in order to feel better. Perhaps they can prompt you to access that? Write down the name of anyone who you feel would be a good supporter in that role.

....

....

....

....

....

Your doctor will usually be a key figure in your support plan. You may have been seeing them periodically throughout this treatment. If you need support, remember that they are there to offer medical advice and they should also be able to refer you, as needed, to expert health professionals.

Your doctor's name

....

....

Your doctor's telephone number

....

....

Finally, make a note of any organisations from the Further resources that you may want to contact should you need any further support. I would suggest that you contact them when you are well and at your best, just so that you are sure that they are the right people to reach out to if you are having a lapse or relapse.

....

....

....

....

....

Congratulations!

We have come an awful long way on this journey

together. I am really pleased that you have managed to complete GET and almost reach the end of this book. Take a moment to think about the progress that you have made towards your goals. The journey may not have been easy. The progress that you have made is down to you! I have just provided you with some tools to allow you to help yourself. I have given you the hammer, wood and nails. You have built the table. With these tools, you can build other tables in the future. Be proud of what you have achieved. Perhaps you can apply some of these principles to other areas of your life to help you to achieve other goals? In life, generally speaking, approaching is a much better strategy for solving problems than avoiding.

This relapse prevention section will help you to keep hold of this progress. It will alert you when to put the necessary tools back into action if that situation arises. This book will always be here if you need it again.

In the next section, we return to Sarah and Azid's stories. They will let us know how they used CBT self-help to get on top of their fears. Some people write down their own story in the way that Sarah and Azid have told theirs. It is then a reminder of what they have achieved. Others may write a short-er letter to themselves to celebrate their progress.

Perhaps you could write your story in this kind of way after reading their recovery stories? You could write this as if it were a letter to yourself in the future, rather like a paper time capsule. Pieces of writing like this can also be added to the toolkit if you wish. You can then reread them as part of your wellbeing reviews, adding to them every so often as needed.

Remember that I have also provided you with a section at the back of the book which has some additional blank worksheets and the details of some organisations that may be of help.

You should now have all of the tools that you need to keep your fears in check in the future. I wish you well.

RECOVERY STORIES

Sarah's story

Sarah is the homemaker whom you met on page 36. She was experiencing a phobia that was linked to spiders. She used graded exposure therapy (GET) to feel better. Here is Sarah's recovery story. Remember that more details of her phobia and her 'ladder' are on pages 72 and 78. Although Sarah's situation is different from your own, reading about her experience may help you to understand more about your phobia and how to carry out GET.

" I always remember being afraid of spiders. My dad used to take us to castles. The dungeons used to worry me. They were dark and dingy. You never know what creepy-crawlies would be lurking in those places. I worried that there would be cobwebs there. I remember that when Mum was alive she wasn't fond of them either. One Christmas my cousin brought over a big furry toy spider. He startled my mother with it and Mum screamed and got quite angry. That was not like Mum at all.

The other kids at school found out that I was scared of them. One boy used to catch them at lunchtime and tease me with them. One time he hid one in my bag. I was petrified. I couldn't go near it. In the end the teacher got it out of my bag for me when she saw I was close to tears. The fear never went away completely, but I left all of that childhood stuff behind I guess. As I got older, I didn't have to worry about people teasing me so much. We all had more important things to think about in secondary school.

When I left school, I remember moving into my first flat. I always kept the places I lived in immaculate. I imagined that spiders would be attracted to dark, dusty places. I remember cleaning quite a bit of the time.

Things settled even more when I got together with Mike. He was my first proper boyfriend back then.

At the start, he was my knight in shining armour. If there was a spider in the flat I could just ask Mike to get rid of it. He seemed to take pride in rescuing me! I didn't have to deal with them as much then. I was working as well, so when we were at home we were usually together. I remember feeling good during those times. If Mike wasn't around, I could just call Dad. Dad lives a couple streets away and so he could just pop round. If he was out, Cheryl, my neighbour on the left, would come and use a cup and a piece of card to catch them. She doesn't seem to be that afraid of them at all.

Then baby Jack came along. I was always worried about his safety. It was such a difficult birth. We were terrified that we would lose him. When he started crawling he was into everything. I always had to keep an eye on him. Of course, I spent more time at home then without Mike, it was just me and Jack. I seemed to be really stressed after the birth. Mike said that I became more anxious. He thought that I was always worrying. When we broke up, I felt even more vulnerable. I didn't have my knight in shining armour anymore. It was just me and Jack. Of course, Dad and Cheryl were around as well if I needed them.

Things seemed to be worse in the late summer and autumn. The spiders seem to be everywhere then. They come out in force – in the garden, in the house;

even in the car. At times I worried that I would swerve off the road if a spider was in the car! Things seemed to get on top of me and I couldn't cope. I couldn't just walk away from spider situations anymore as I had Jack to look after now. Then there was that time when he had a spider on his cot. I was hysterical. I couldn't go near it! It was a big long-legged one just sitting there. What if something would have happened to Jack? I felt so helpless. Of course, Dad came round straight away when I rang him, but that isn't the point. I'm Jack's mum. I should be able to deal with these things. When that happened, I thought enough is enough. I need to get things sorted.

That's when I went to see Dr Brown. He asked me a bit about what had been going on for me. When I had been in to see him before it had been just to do with Jack. This time we spoke more about me. I got a bit teary in the appointment. I told him about the spider and the cot, and also Mike leaving. He said that it was understandable that my anxiety would be worse as I had more going on and less support in my life. He suggested that I look at a book called *How to Beat Fears and Phobias One Step at a Time*. He said that a while back another of his patients had a phobia and they found the book really helpful. He had a list of books that he printed out from the computer and circled that one for me. He said that they might have a copy in my local library. He asked to see me again in a month's time. I thought that this would be plenty of time to get hold of the book and see what it said.

Initially I wasn't sure at all about 'self-help'. One way or another I had been trying to cope with this fear for much of my life. I remember when there was a smaller spider in the kitchen near the door, Mike encouraged me to try to trap it with a glass and a piece of card and throw it out the door. He said that it would be easy. It wasn't! What could this book offer that Mike couldn't? Anyway, I managed to get a copy out of the library. They had a whole section on 'wellbeing'. The book was in there. When I got home, I really got into the book. I was really interested to learn that my fear was just a normal reaction really. That was a relief for me. I felt more sane right then! It explained things in a way that allowed me to see the patterns in my life. When I saw those, I knew what I had to do, but wasn't sure if I could actually do it. The first half of the book was easier. It wasn't very nice thinking about my fears, but in the first couple of chapters I just had to learn about them by doing some written exercises. I realised that it wasn't just fear, it was my thinking and acting as well that were part of the problem. It was all connected.

The book asked me to produce a ladder [Sarah's ladder is on page 78]. I had to think of all the things that set off my fear. It was really difficult to think of all of these things, but I just took my time. I eventually got there. Then came the most stressful bit, the exposure! Cheryl was a godsend. She came over with dead spiders, live spiders, all sorts. She knew I had this problem and so I told her about the book and the treatment. She was great. She was there 100 per cent for me. I remember when I had to have a live spider on me, Cheryl would trap it under a glass beaker and put it on me whilst it was under the glass. On the first practice, she waited there with me the whole time. Dad would come over and play with Jack in the garden while all this was going on. I soon got confident that it couldn't escape from the glass and after that she went back to her place during the practice sessions to get on with stuff and came back to take the spider off of me when I was ready. She kept poking her head round the door every so often just to see how it was all going. We used to have a cuppa at the end of the practices and that was great. In a way I think my phobia brought us much closer together. Eventually, I was able to allow the spider to crawl on me without being trapped in the glass.

I had my watch on the table during the practices and wrote down the time every five minutes. I was really surprised to see my anxiety come down after a while. That had never happened like that before. I never gave it a chance. The record sheets were really useful 'cause I could then see the pattern of it getting easier and easier as the weeks went on. That gave me the confidence to try the steps higher up in my ladder. I was amazed. After six weeks, I was actually able to have a spider crawl on me. I could trap it and set it loose in the garden. It was still not pleasant, but I could do it! I really regained my confidence. I felt that I didn't need anyone to help me anymore with spiders.

The book talked about 'red flags'. I realised that if a spider hadn't been around for a while and then one turned up, I was more tempted to ring Cheryl or Dad to come and fetch it out. That urge was an early warning sign for me. When that happened, not only would I force myself to take the spider out and release it, I would catch it again, bring it in and repeat this over and over until it felt 'doable'.

If I keep on top of this, it can only be better all around. When he gets older, Jack is bound to want to play in the garden, build forts in the bushes, play in tree houses, those kinds of things. I would be gutted if I couldn't do that with him.*"*

Azid's story

You met Azid on page 36. After nearly having an accident whilst driving on a road bridge, he started avoiding them because of the unpleasant symptoms in his body that he started to experience. After seeing his doctor, Dr Chen, he was referred to a psychological wellbeing practitioner and they began to work through this self-help book together. Here is Azid's story. Remember that his ladder is on page 80.

" The experience on the bridge was terrifying. I remember it like it was yesterday. It was such a windy day. I remember having doubts about going over the bridge in the first place. Once on the bridge, I could see the lorry drivers struggling to control their wagons. The empty high-sided lorries were the worst. You could see them swinging in the wind.

I was going quite slow to take it easy and a lorry came past me on the inner lane of the bridge. As it went past the wind caught the back of it and it swung towards me. I slammed on the brakes and it missed me by inches. As I braked, my car pulled to one side and for a moment I thought I was going to crash into the side of the bridge. My heart was pounding out of my chest. My palms were wet. Luckily there was no one directly behind me or they could have gone into me and pushed me over the side.

I drove home really slowly, and I was really in a daze. What if I had gone over the side? What a near miss! I would never have survived the fall. Images went through my mind like a film, where cars went over and over the sides of bridges, except this time it was me in my car. That could have been me!

The images seemed to fade over the next few days, but I was left with huge anxiety whilst going over that bridge. Every time I went over it felt like an endurance. I dreaded that bit of the commute. Somehow the more anxious I got, the more I felt that something bad was about to happen. Eventually, I thought: 'Why put yourself through it. It's just not worth it.' I would rather spend an extra thirty minutes travelling if it meant that I could relax on the journey. I guess that was the mistake. In the end, I had no choice. I don't think I could have gone over the bridge to save my own life. I seemed to build it up so much in my mind.

Soon I was struggling with other bridges as well. It all just seemed to creep up on me. I was feeling anxious on them too and so again I just thought: 'Why bother when there is another option?' Before I knew it, I was finding the practicalities of always going around bridges rather than over them really difficult to handle. I was leaving the house earlier and arriving home later. My wife eventually said that I needed to see the doctor about the problem. She seemed to be more frustrated with the problem than I was!

I contacted Dr Chen the next day and she could fit me in on the day after. She asked me about the incident and I told her about the changes that happened in my body and in my driving afterwards. Dr Chen said that she thought that I may be experiencing a phobia and asked me whether I would be happy to see John who was a psychological wellbeing practitioner (PWP) who worked nearby. I had never heard of a PWP, but the doctor said that they could teach me skills to help me to get better. That sounded great to me as I really just don't feel comfortable taking medication unless it is absolutely necessary. John phoned me the next day when I was on the road and I arranged to see him on Fridays as I knew I would always be local then.

Two weeks later I went to the appointment to see John. The first meeting seemed more of an opportunity for him to get to know about my problem. Towards the end, he discussed a few things about phobias with me and said that he recommended a CBT self-help programme. John said that this would be the best treatment for me. That was fine by me as I like to be in control of what's going on. Self-help seemed as if it would be right up my street.

John said that he could help me to use the book by checking in with me weekly. He offered me a choice of doing this by telephone or by me coming in to see him. I decided to come in and see him as there was nowhere very private in the office. When I got home from the appointment, I ordered the book from an online retailer and I started to read it after it arrived the next day. I could see how my phobia had developed. The book seemed to be saying that I had been conditioned by the fright that I had. Thinking back though, I also realised that Dad was pretty worried about heights and bridges. He used to tense up and go quiet when he drove over them. I wondered whether that had affected me in some way.

I read about the four conditions of exposure and could not think how my trips over bridges could be 'prolonged'. At my slowest, I think I could get across the longest of them in under two minutes. John suggested a solution to this. As soon as possible, once over the bridge, I should turn around and go back over it again, repeating the process until my fear had reduced by 50 per cent. If anyone had followed me they would have thought that I was mad, but in fact it worked really well. I made sure to turn the radio off as I wondered whether this would count as a distraction – the book said not to have any of those. I did the exposure sessions in the evening. My wife was just happy that I was getting some help and so she was fine with it. In fact, when I wasn't so confident about starting the process, she even agreed to come along with me as a passenger for a few practice sessions.

The sessions with John were great; I felt really supported. He just kept pushing me on, but not in a bad way. If I had any questions he always knew the answer, but he let me have control over the whole process. It took a bit longer than I expected, but after a couple of months I was back to travelling over the bridge where I had my near miss. John had been asking me to fill in questionnaires for each session with him and he said that by that point, according to my ratings, I was pretty much back to normal. We arranged one last session where John went through relapse prevention with me. This was really about staying well now I had got this far. John helped me think of some early warning signs such as making excuses not to use the bridges again or arranging to do things at the weekend just to the north of the Tyne, so we didn't have to cross the river. John explained that I shouldn't give into these urges and it made sense – I could see that giving in had created the problem in the first place.

My red flags

My early warning signs are:

Asking my wife if we can take her car (she would then drive)

Making suggestions to do things just this side of the river

Organising my week so that I have bridge-free days

Avoiding some bridges on bad weather days

Using the tunnel more than I need to

Avoiding using the outer lane on larger bridges

John and I set up a wellbeing action plan at the end of our sessions so that I could keep an eye on things, but it was my wife who noticed that I was tending to avoid the high bridges again on windy days. So, I restarted some practice sessions to cover that, just to get my confidence back again.

My wellbeing review

Review date:

1st June

What have my symptoms been like over the last month?

Not too bad. Just the odd twinge occasionally going over the Redheugh Bridge. I am not avoiding it though, and I try to go over it every day in the week just to monitor how I am doing and to keep up my confidence.

Reading through my red flags list, have I had any experiences that have concerned me?

No, last month I had noticed that I was avoiding the bridge on windy days but this month this has been much better. I have asked my wife to keep an eye on whether I am asking her to drive to avoid bridges and she doesn't think so, we just share the driving pretty evenly at the weekends. I did use the tunnel a couple of times over the last month but that was just because it was quicker, so I am happy about that.

Do I need to take any action now to keep on top of my fear?

Not this month. I will continue to use the Redheugh Bridge every day in the week if possible as I think that is a good system of keeping a check on things.

If so, what will be helpful to use in my toolkit?

Not needed this month, but I will continue to ask my wife whether she notices any red flags every week.

What do I need to do and when am I going to do it?

N/A

The date of my next review is:

6th July

As we finished up, John said that he thought that I had done really well over the treatment. I was really chuffed with myself as well. I was aware of the patterns that fed the problem and the patterns that were the solution. I have come a long way over these few months and I now have the ability again to drive wherever I want to. Although I still have the odd niggle, for the most part it feels as if I have now been set free from my fear. "

FURTHER RESOURCES

My goals for feeling better

Goal 1: ....

....

....

I can do this now   (Today's date___/___/___)
(circle a number):

   0   1   2   3   4   5   6

Not at all   Occasionally   Often   Any time

One-month rerating   (date___/___/___)
(circle a number):

   0   1   2   3   4   5   6

Not at all   Occasionally   Often   Any time

Two-month rerating   (date___/___/___)
(circle a number):

   0   1   2   3   4   5   6

Not at all   Occasionally   Often   Any time

Three-month rerating   (date___/___/___)
(circle a number):

0   1   2   3   4   5   6
Not at all   Occasionally   Often   Any time

Goal 2: ....

....

....

I can do this now   (Today's date___/___/___)
(circle a number):

0   1   2   3   4   5   6
Not at all   Occasionally   Often   Any time

One-month rerating   (date___/___/___)
(circle a number):

0   1   2   3   4   5   6
Not at all   Occasionally   Often   Any time

Two-month rerating   (date___/___/___)
(circle a number):

0   1   2   3   4   5   6
Not at all   Occasionally   Often   Any time

Three-month rerating   (date___/___/___)
(circle a number):

0	1	2	3	4	5	6
Not at all		Occasionally		Often	Any time	

Goal 3: ....

....

....

I can do this now   (Today's date___/___/___)
(circle a number):

0	1	2	3	4	5	6
Not at all		Occasionally		Often	Any time	

One-month rerating   (date___/___/___)
(circle a number):

0	1	2	3	4	5	6
Not at all		Occasionally		Often	Any time	

Two-month rerating   (date___/___/___)
(circle a number):

0	1	2	3	4	5	6
Not at all		Occasionally		Often	Any time	

Three-month rerating   (date___/___/___)
(circle a number):

   0   1   2   3   4   5   6

  Not at all   Occasionally   Often   Any time

Your ladder

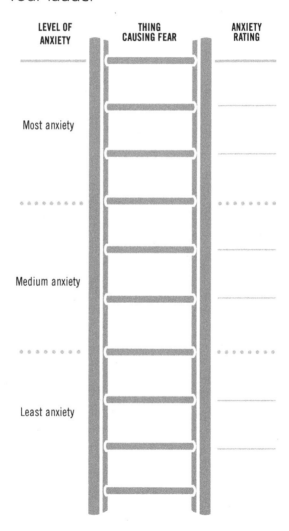

Your ladder

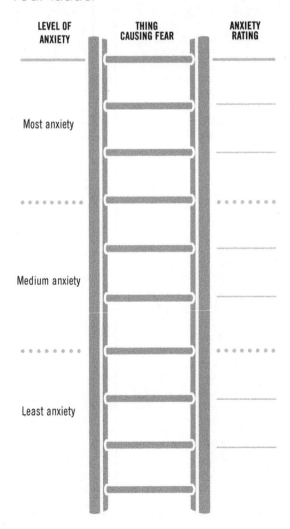

Facing your fears record sheet

Exposure task	Details of your feared thing for this session:

Date and time of planned practice sessions		Exposure anxiety ratings (0–100)			
		Start of session	Highest level	End of session	Duration of session
	Session 1				

	Session 2	Session 3	Session 4	Session 5	Session 6	Session 7	Session 8

Facing your fears record sheet

Exposure task	Details of your feared thing for this session:			
		Exposure anxiety ratings (0–100)		
Date and time of planned practice sessions		Start of session	Highest level	End of session	Duration of session
	Session 1				

Session 2	Session 3	Session 4	Session 5	Session 6	Session 7	Session 8

Facing your fears record sheet

Exposure task	Details of your feared thing for this session:

Date and time of planned practice sessions		Exposure anxiety ratings (0–100)			
		Start of session	Highest level	End of session	Duration of session
	Session 1				

Session 2	Session 3	Session 4	Session 5	Session 6	Session 7	Session 8

Facing your fears record sheet

Exposure task	Details of your feared thing for this session:

Date and time of planned practice sessions		Exposure anxiety ratings (0–100)			
		Start of session	Highest level	End of session	Duration of session
	Session 1				

Session 2	Session 3	Session 4	Session 5	Session 6	Session 7	Session 8

Facing your fears record sheet

Exposure task	Details of your feared thing for this session:			
		Exposure anxiety ratings (0–100)		
		Start of session	Highest level	End of session	Duration of session
Date and time of planned practice sessions					
	Session 1				

Session 2	Session 3	Session 4	Session 5	Session 6	Session 7	Session 8

Facing your fears record sheet

Exposure task	Details of your feared thing for this session:			
Date and time of planned practice sessions		Exposure anxiety ratings (0–100)		
		Start of session	Highest level	End of session	Duration of session
	Session 1				

Session 2	Session 3	Session 4	Session 5	Session 6	Session 7	Session 8

Facing your fears record sheet

Exposure task	Details of your feared thing for this session:			
		Exposure anxiety ratings (0–100)		
Date and time of planned practice sessions	Start of session	Highest level	End of session	Duration of session
Session 1				

Session 2	Session 3	Session 4	Session 5	Session 6	Session 7	Session 8

Facing your fears record sheet

Exposure task	Details of your feared thing for this session:			
		Exposure anxiety ratings (0–100)		
		Start of session	Highest level	End of session	Duration of session
Date and time of planned practice sessions				
	Session 1				

Session 2	Session 3	Session 4	Session 5	Session 6	Session 7	Session 8

Facing your fears record sheet

Exposure task	Details of your feared thing for this session:			
		Exposure anxiety ratings (0–100)		
Date and time of planned practice sessions	Start of session	Highest level	End of session	Duration of session
Session 1				

Session 2	Session 3	Session 4	Session 5	Session 6	Session 7	Session 8

Facing your fears record sheet

Exposure task		Details of your feared thing for this session:			
Date and time of planned practice sessions			Exposure anxiety ratings (0–100)		
		Start of session	Highest level	End of session	Duration of session
	Session 1				

Session 2	Session 3	Session 4	Session 5	Session 6	Session 7	Session 8

Facing your fears record sheet

Exposure task	Details of your feared thing for this session:

Date and time of planned practice sessions	Exposure anxiety ratings (0–100)			
	Start of session	Highest level	End of session	Duration of session
Session 1				

Session 2	Session 3	Session 4	Session 5	Session 6	Session 7	Session 8

My wellbeing review

Review date:

What have my symptoms been like over the last month?

Reading through my red flags list, have I had any experiences that have concerned me?

Do I need to take any action now to keep on top of my fear?

If so, what will be helpful to use in my toolkit?

What do I need to do and when am I going to do it?

The date of my next review is:

My wellbeing review

Review date:

What have my symptoms been like over the last month?

Reading through my red flags list, have I had any experiences that have concerned me?

Do I need to take any action now to keep on top of my fear?

If so, what will be helpful to use in my toolkit?

What do I need to do and when am I going to do it?

The date of my next review is:

My wellbeing review

Review date:

What have my symptoms been like over the last month?

Reading through my red flags list, have I had any experiences that have concerned me?

Do I need to take any action now to keep on top of my fear?

If so, what will be helpful to use in my toolkit?

What do I need to do and when am I going to do it?

The date of my next review is:

My wellbeing review

Review date:

What have my symptoms been like over the last month?

Reading through my red flags list, have I had any experiences that have concerned me?

Do I need to take any action now to keep on top of my fear?

If so, what will be helpful to use in my toolkit?

What do I need to do and when am I going to do it?

The date of my next review is:

My wellbeing review

Review date:

What have my symptoms been like over the last month?

Reading through my red flags list, have I had any experiences that have concerned me?

Do I need to take any action now to keep on top of my fear?

If so, what will be helpful to use in my toolkit?

What do I need to do and when am I going to do it?

The date of my next review is:

My wellbeing review

Review date:

What have my symptoms been like over the last month?

Reading through my red flags list, have I had any experiences that have concerned me?

Do I need to take any action now to keep on top of my fear?

If so, what will be helpful to use in my toolkit?

What do I need to do and when am I going to do it?

The date of my next review is:

Further information

The National Health Service (in the UK)

The UK NHS website has a summary of useful information about phobias. The relevant webpage is:

https://www.nhs.uk/conditions/phobias

This page https://www.nhs.uk/conditions/phobias/treatment includes a video which describes how to refer yourself in England for psychological therapies and tells you what to expect.

The website also has details of other anxiety conditions. Reading through these should help you to confirm whether your difficulties are symptoms of a phobia (rather than a different anxiety condition). It will also allow you to determine whether you might be experiencing another anxiety condition as well. The relevant webpage is:

https://www.nhs.uk/common-health-questions/lifestyle/do-i-have-an-anxiety-disorder

You can find a psychological treatment service in England via this page:

https://www.nhs.uk/service-search/find-a-psychological-therapies-service

Remember that your doctor will also be able to discuss these things with you as well as support you in your CBT self-help. In England, they will also be able to refer you to a psychological wellbeing practitioner who is specially trained to support you in this way. Remember to keep your doctor informed of both the treatments that you are involved in and all the health professionals that you are in contact with.

Most people with a psychological problem feel at times as if they can't continue in this way. However, if you have suicidal thoughts and are planning to act on those thoughts, I strongly recommend that you access support from a crisis team. You should be able to access a local crisis team in the UK through your GP, your local accident and emergency department or the police. From this web page you can download information about these teams and how to access them: https://www.rethink.org/advice-and-information/living-with-mental-illness/treatment-and-support/crisis-teams

Scotland, Ireland and Wales are not part of the IAPT programme and so currently there are no self-referral systems into mental health services in these countries. You can access treatment by visiting your doctor.

Voluntary organisations

Samaritans. They can be contacted by telephone, email or in person at one of their branches. They can offer emotional support by providing a neutral, sympathetic listening ear to people who are in distress. The instructions for contacting them are provided on this webpage: https://www.samaritans. org/how-we-can-help/contact-samaritan

Mind. This charity also has some useful information about phobias on this webpage: https://www.mind. org.uk/information-support/types-of-mental-health-problems/phobias. They also offer some advice for family and friends of those who are experiencing a phobia.

Groups. Some charities may offer more 'hands-on' support, for instance via groups. I have not had any personal contact with these organisations or those who have attended these groups, but highlight that this form of support is available in the UK and some other countries, for instance: www.topuk.org/ topuk-groups

There are some other charities listed on this webpage: https://www.babcp.com/public/Accessing-CBT.aspx

The Scottish Association for Mental Health (https:// www.samh.org.uk/find-help) supports those in Scotland who experience a range of mental health

difficulties. Their website has some additional resources listed on it including a confidential helpline:
https://breathingspace.scot

Time to Change Wales (https://www.timetochange
wales.org.uk/en/need-help) includes   details of
some general mental health support services for the
Welsh. A confidential help line resource is provided
by the Mental Health Helpline for Wales: http://
www.callhelpline.org.uk

Private sector

I have mentioned earlier in the book that you can
find a private CBT therapist (who will charge a fee
for each session) via this website: https://www.bab
cp.com/public/Accessing-CBT.aspx

ACKNOWLEDGEMENTS

Paul Farrand and Marie Chellingsworth are the originators of this series. They wrote the first three titles. I have continued to use their structure and format for this book.

CBT self-help books have been published for several decades and health professionals have been supporting people in their use over this time. However, Dave Richards and Mark Whyte first published information about 'low intensity CBT' and the new role of the PWP in the English NHS.

Aside from the editorial team at Little, Brown, Theresa Marrinan has commented on a draft of this book.

I would also like to thank my partner, Danna, for her comments, proof-reading skills and support in my writing of this book.

INDEX

Note: page numbers in **bold** refer to diagrams.

9/10/20